FREE WILL BAPTIST
GUIDE
for new
believers

JOURNEY OF A LIFETIME FOR NEW MEMBERS AND BELIEVERS

GENERAL EDITOR RON HUNTER JR.

randall house
114 Bush Rd | Nashville, TN 37217 | randallhouse.com

© 2012 by Randall House

Published by Randall House
114 Bush Road
Nashville, TN 37217

Printed in the United States of America

ISBN-10: 0892656603

ISBN-13: 9780892656608

INTRODUCTION

BEFORE BEGINNING YOUR HIKE

You must prepare for hikes, especially long ones. As a new believer or a veteran Christ-follower, your journey occurs in good and bad weather, through easy and difficult terrain and your progression depends on your preparation. What do you pack for a hike that turns into the journey of a lifetime? This book, along with your local church, provides knowledge, wisdom, and a foundation upon which you can build. The GPS replaces the older compass but you still plot your direction on a map even if in digital form.

The following chapters provide an orderly approach to map your walk as a believer. Twelve chapters, twelve lessons, and fourteen authors each selected for their unique insight to the topic will help you become a stronger believer and Christ follower. Many thanks are owed to Craig Priestly, Emily White Youree, Paul Harrison, Danny Conn, and Randy Ledbetter for due diligence in specific edits each of you made. It was a pleasure to work with each of the authors who collectively worked together to produce one unique work.

In 1678, John Bunyan wrote the best selling Christian allegory entitled Pilgrim's Progress. The writer's approach of weaving Scripture and protestant theology into a story became refreshingly popular as he encouraged people on a path toward Heaven. The *Free Will Baptist Guide for New Believers* presents a modern day Pilgrim's Progress for Free Will Baptists. As your pastor or teacher leads you through this study, read the supporting Scripture, spend time in prayer, and grab the recommended resources.

Put into your pack the resources needed and walk with others going the same way. God's desires you to finish well. Before every finish line is a track, course, or path to cover. How you share the path with other Christians may indicate how well prepared you are for the journey of a lifetime. You met Christ at the trailhead and He promised you would not travel alone. It is time to begin your hike.

Ron Hunter Jr.

Table of Contents

A Note To Leaders

Visit www.randallhouse.com for a free Leader's Guide.

This is the hike of your life, and the path you choose makes all the difference.

One path follows the Trailblazer, the God-man, Jesus Christ (Hebrews 6:20). It is a journey designed to unmake and remake you, expose your darkest secrets of sin, but then bury them in His grace, while outfitting you for heaven. Jesus is a confident, happy, and encouraging leader, but He carries His scars. Sometimes He weeps. From this alone, you know His trail is not for the faint-hearted. Read Matthew 7:14.

The other path is foot-worn and familiar. It slopes downhill and out of sight. This path holds bitter reminders of your failed attempts at morality, at quelling fear and despair, and at achieving contentment by ambition, purchase, or pleasure. Read Matthew 7:13.

CHOOSING THE PATH: HOW DID YOU RECEIVE SALVATION?

You were on the same path your entire life, and you knew it was a road to nowhere. It doubled back, putting you in the same predicaments over and over. Sometimes it was so wide and indistinct that you wondered if it was a path at all. As the inescapable questions of life confronted you, no answers were found there. Is there a God? Does He care about me? How can I know Him? What does He want me to do?

There was grave danger on the path that leads to a destination without Jesus Christ. There were so many damaged people around you, covered with self-inflicted wounds, floundering in despair, or addicted to whatever distractions they could find. If something had not changed, you knew that you too would fall victim to spiritual death and physical dangers, and at the end of your life you would only be *more lost*—with no purpose, direction, or hope. This was and is the path that leads to hell.

At some point in your recent past, Jesus appeared on your path, although you had been walking away from Him. Somehow He got your attention. Maybe a friend pointed you to Christ with a word, a deed, or a prayer, and now Jesus is pointing at a new life of purpose, friendship with Him, and future blessings.

As you listened to Him, saw His truth, and trusted His Name, you had an incredible realization: *your direction was your decision.* You had never before even *considered* changing paths. You were so damaged that you could not have imagined being whole again—you had simply accepted your fate. You did not know how to change. You had tried to change before, but you always ended up going the same direction, even more damaged. No matter what you tried—anger management, marriage counseling, doing good deeds, attending church, or New Year's resolutions—the same outcome always resulted.

That was good, because it led you to your second important realization: *you were not equipped to change direction on your own.* Becoming a Christ follower requires accepting your own inability to go anywhere but *down.* His Path—we call it *salvation*—requires accepting your limitations and depending on Jesus Christ's limitlessness.

Following Christ requires personal faith—not just the kind that believes *something,* but the kind that believes *Someone.* Trust is hard and frustrating. It makes you vulnerable. Trust is risky because it puts someone else in charge. Trust means that you keep on following while having some *very* reasonable doubts.

You only knew how to walk the *previous* path, that is, how to depend on your own cleverness or ability to fix your life. All your attempts to change direction had failed. You needed a new life and that meant a new direction, following a new leader. It would help to have some idea of just what this involves.

Well, you're fortunate. Jesus is only too happy to give you a full orientation for your change to the God-life. He left it for you in Paul's letter to the Church in Rome, what we call the book of Romans in the New Testament portion of the Bible.

Following Jesus began where you were: *sin.* Everyone walking Christ's path must first deal with his or her sin debt (Romans 3:23). No matter who you are, we all blaze the same trail: *sin.* No matter how hard you try or how many resolutions you make, your sin path takes you away from God and deeper into a life of self-focused and self-interested self-worship. Out of a sense of survival and self-preservation, you choose selfishness over generosity, deception over disclosure, and defensive hate over vulnerable love (Romans 3:9-20).

Sin is the reason Jesus had to *intervene*. On your sin path, you did not even desire to find Jesus (Romans 3:11-12). Furthermore, He was going up a hill that was too steep to climb under your own power (Romans 6:23; Ephesians 2:8-9). Besides, you were *lost*. You couldn't run fast enough or climb hard enough to be *un-lost*.

When someone is lost in the woods, he or she tends to panic. That person is conscious of the real dangers, and imagines a few more. "Fight or flight" kicks in.

Before Christ became your life leader, you had no one to fight but yourself, and running away faster only left you more lost and your life more complicated. You only became more bewildered as you faced everyday problems. *Jesus had to blaze a path to you* through sin before you could follow Him.

It is Jesus' path, and only He can lead the way. Jesus intentionally left the safety, plenty, and honor of His home in heaven, set out into the wilderness of sin, and walked our path—maintaining His holiness and perfection at all times (Hebrews 4:15). Essentially, He came looking for the lost without becoming lost Himself (1 Peter 2:22). He gave up everything and died the death you deserved on the cross. He defeated sin as well as physical and spiritual death when God resurrected Him from the grave. Jesus established the path to eternal life and returned to heaven so that you can now follow Him (Romans 5:6-10). No one but God could accomplish this. He rescued you from a trajectory to hell, and you get to live eternally. Salvation isn't *easy*, but Jesus made it *accessible* through your faith and confession of sin (Romans 10:8-10).

Jesus made this path available for you, whether you choose it or not. Imagine how much He must care about you: He joined you on your path, conquered the sin, and made a way of escape out of your sin-life, with no guarantee that you would even respond to Him. It would make sense to do that for someone who loved Him, but He did it for strangers, vagabonds, rebels, and sinners (Romans 5:6-10).

Jesus took all your burdens and threw them away. Your life had been more difficult because of the sin and guilt you carried. Your sin burdens (selfishness, distrust, guilt, etc.) were so heavy that you were exhausted and empty from either bearing them or hiding them. Climbing to righteousness was impossible.

When Jesus was crucified He took your sin upon Himself, and His resurrection placed His sinlessness upon you when you placed your trust in Him (Romans 5:8-11). He took your burdens in spite of the horrible things He and you both know you did, and in spite of the insults and curses you hurled in His direction when the burdens crushed you. *You couldn't carry the load yourself any more than you could have found salvation by yourself.*

He did not *help* you with your sinful burdens; *He took them away from you and discarded them.* He bought you with His blood when He died on the cross. If you insist on carrying your sin guilt, you cannot follow Him (Isaiah 53:4-9).

Your sins were buried with Jesus, and He left them in the tomb when He resurrected. If you pick them up again, you are hauling a corpse around with you (Romans 6:1-7, Galatians 2:20). While Christians are not perfect so you will still sin, you goal is to please Christ and live a life honoring to Him (2 Corinthians 5:17). A Christian who resumes his or her former sinful lifestyle looks *more* sinful than someone who has never known Christ (2 Peter 2:18-22).

His trail is open to anyone who trusts Him. Everyone is lost in sin, and anyone can be rescued from it (Romans 10:11-13). Jesus didn't die on the cross to provide salvation only to dangle it before us and refuse to grant it. God gave His Son to die in your place so He no longer would be separated from you by sin. Jesus' death maintains God's justice towards sin while forgiving us all (Romans 3:25-26). He sent His Son so that anyone who trusted in the work of His Son on the cross could have a relationship with God and be able to spend eternity with Him in heaven (John 14:6, John 3:16). Jesus blazed His trail to be followed to heaven, and He cuts through the chaos to our sin path so we can access it. Salvation wasn't easy, but God made it accessible.

JOINING THE HIKE: Who can be saved?

Describe your life before deciding to walk with Christ on this new hike and compare it to having Him walk with you now.

_____

_____

_____

Read Romans 3:23, 6:23 and Ephesians 2:8-9 and tell what you did to earn salvation?

_____

_____

Have you made the decision to be a Christ follower on this journey?

❏ *Yes*   ❏ *No*   *(If no, you can read the following verses to show how you can accept the free gift of salvation to become a Christian. John 3:16, Romans 3:23, Romans 6:23, Romans 5:8 and Romans 10:9, 10, 13.)*

✎ Every human being was created in the image of God. That means you have the intellect, emotions, and will to understand, react to, and accept Christ's forgiving work. Since God created you with these attributes, He expects you to use them. The most critical utilization of these attributes occurs when Jesus intervenes in your path and points the way to salvation through His death and resurrection.

Although there is almost no limit to the depth of humanity's sinful imaginations, we still retain the image of God (James 3:8-10). This image includes the intellect to decide whether or not we believe God's plan of salvation, the emotion to decide whether or not we regard His mercy as necessary, and the will to accept His grace to save us from our sin and restore God's image within us all contribute to humanity's freedom to choose to receive God's rescue. This *free will* is how we *Free Will Baptists* got our name. God has not predetermined those whom He would save and those whom He would not save; He will save whoever responds to His salvation plan (Romans 10:13). You have the opportunity to follow Him when the Holy Spirit invites you. Jesus died for all, but when God invites, you don't have to listen. Your direction is your decision.

God's Word emphasizes that He has not limited salvation's offer (Titus 2:11; Hebrews 2:9; 1 Timothy 2:6; Isaiah 45:22; 2 Peter 3:9; 2 Corinthians 5:14-15; 1 Timothy 4:10). Anyone desiring to follow Jesus away from his or her sin is enabled by the Holy Spirit to do so.

STUMBLING STONES:
What makes Jesus' path so difficult to follow?

As a boy, I attended a church picnic in a large, wooded park. When we played hide-and-seek, the person who was "it" counted to 10 very quickly. The first time he counted, all of us were still in plain sight when he opened his eyes, so we decided that he should count to 100. He counted even faster so we had to run in order to hide, and I tried to run through the woods to find a good hiding place. If you ever consider running through the woods, I have a one-word recommendation for you: *don't*. I emerged with scraped knees and elbows, and a bloody lip, a hornet sting—all without finding a hiding place. Needless to say, I was "it" next.

Running through the woods is dangerous because forests are full of rocks, potholes, uneven ground, and exposed roots that can and will trip you. These things are even more treacherous when camouflaged by fallen leaves.

Likewise, a number of things conspire to trip you as you follow Jesus:

You aren't out of the woods yet. We see in Scripture people who walked through both physical and spiritual wildernesses. You will face spiritual wildernesses, and you may feel like you are walking through these challenges alone. The good news is that although the wilderness is treacherous, God uses the hardships of life to make you stronger, more durable, and self-controlled (James 1:2-12). God used physical wilderness experiences to shape Abraham (Genesis 12), Moses (Exodus 2—3), David (1 Samuel 17:33-35), John the Baptist (Matthew 3:1), and Paul (Galatians 1:15-17) into the people He created them to be. Jesus chose to go into the wilderness to be prepared for His ministry (Matthew 4:1-11; Mark 1:12-14; Luke 4:1-14). He will likewise strengthen you through your emotional, mental, or spiritual wilderness.

You don't always watch your step. The Bible becomes your GPS or map in dark, disorienting times (Psalm 119:105). Other believers help provide protection in danger (Ecclesiastes 4:11-12; I Thessalonians 5:11, Ephesians 4:25). Taking care not to wear out spiritually keeps you from quitting (Galatians 6:9). But you can ignore all these helps. You may decide to launch out on your own (Luke 15:11-13). If you do declare independence, it won't be long before you run out of friends, food, and fun (Luke 15:14-17). Like the Prodigal Son, you will be lonely, without resources, and ashamed of yourself. Then what happens?

You already know the bad news—you blew it; but the good news is really good: *grace is greater than all our sins.* Grace is what saved you (Ephesians 2:8-10), and grace is what takes you back when you realize you have strayed from God (Luke 15:18-24). God's forgiveness is available for those times when we've failed even after we've accepted Him. He knows better than you how many traps await you on the path *out* of the wilderness of sin. He never stops providing His grace for His children—all we have to do is admit our sin (1 John 1:9) and turn away from it.

You have an enemy. You also have an enemy, Satan, who is determined to bring you back to your sins. Satan will use problems to whisper that Jesus doesn't know what He's doing, that He's leading you into danger, death, and dead ends, or that you shouldn't have to put up with problems anymore, if Jesus is so knowledgeable and powerful. That's when doubt sets in and fear attacks. Remember that God provides *assurance* of our salvation (1John 5:13). It is a *narrow path through the wilderness of sin*—not a tightrope, a maze, or a hall of mirrors.

A lot of the stuff that trips you up is thrown at you intentionally. Jesus warned that whenever His Kingdom is received, Satan arrives to pick at it and extract it if possible (Matthew 13:4, 19). Satan has an evil substitute to hinder or replace for any good thing Jesus does (Matthew 13:24–30).

His tactics not only cause you to wander from the Lord's path, but they are also designed to make you look like (1) a fool for following Jesus or (2) a hypocrite who claims status in Jesus' family for your own prideful or selfish intentions. You will explore more of Satan's tactics in Chapter 8 of this study, but let's look at a couple of his roles as you are getting started.

Ephesians 3:8–10 says we get to become a Christian because of God's grace. Look up the word "Grace" in a dictionary or ask your pastor what this word means, and describe what grace has done for you in the light of Romans 3:23.

_____

_____

_____

_____

James 2:1–12 implies the journey is a hike—not a walk. It will be challenging and at times difficult. What do you see being difficult in the days ahead? (Share these with another Christ follower so they can help you on this hike).

_____

_____

If you have asked Jesus to forgive you of your sins and determined to have a solid relationship with Jesus, have you since doubted if you really are a Christian, Christ follower, or if you are on your way to heaven? (If yes, read 1 John 5:13)

_____

_____

The Compensator

Some parts of the Christian life are enjoyable, like experiencing community with other Christians. Some parts are personally beneficial like receiving support when you're hurting, or obtaining assistance when you're facing crisis. Some parts of it can contribute to pride, like performing music during a worship service. Other parts may require more of you than you desire, like tithing, regular church attendance, or helping someone when you're busy. Other parts may terrify you, like when you first begin to talk to others about Jesus or pray in public. Satan may encourage you to solely rely on your strengths and focus on areas you enjoy, and to ignore the other areas that challenge or frighten you. He attempts to once again convince you that you can earn your place in the family by over-compensating for your weaknesses.

This will not work. The story of salvation teaches us that *doing everything is not enough!* How could you hope to be a faithful Christ follower when you pick and choose what commands you will obey? You needed Jesus to save you in the first place because you were too weak to save yourself. Do not be fooled into thinking that even though you couldn't work hard enough to save yourself, you can somehow work hard enough to *keep* yourself in the family of God. Jesus disagreed; He taught that even when you have done your *whole duty* it *still* isn't enough to earn what grace gives (Luke 17:10). Embrace all aspects of the Christian life in freedom, knowing that your performance does not contribute to your status as a child of God.

The Critic

Hard work cannot earn salvation, but obedience is *evidence* of salvation (James 2:14-26). Still yet, Satan encourages some followers of Christ to criticize others and create a false comfort by measuring the commitment of others against their own. How long do they pray? How many Bible chapters do they read daily? Do they read through the Bible every year? How many times do they share the Gospel each week? How do they dress? Do they watch too much television (that is, "more than I (the judge) watch")?

This is discouraging to other believers, and that's why Satan promotes it. It is risky to use quantitative measurements to holiness. Not everyone follows Jesus at the same pace or is as far along in the journey.

You also have Jesus. Troubles aren't *all* you have ahead of you. You have Jesus, and He has promised that He will always be with you (Matthew 28:20). Here are some ways to assure yourself that you are following Him faithfully:

Be logical. Think things through in light of what God has told you in His Word. If Jesus died to conquer sin and bring you forgiveness, why wouldn't He be willing to take care of you? He knows what He's doing. You can have complete confidence in your successful journey because Jesus not only *knows* the beginning and the end; but He *is* also the beginning and the end (Hebrews 12:2; Revelation 1:8, 21:6). He didn't save you to leave you. He wants to see you in heaven.

Be a looker. The Christian walk is tough when we don't pay attention . . . so *pay attention* to spiritual reality! The Holy Spirit equips you with a spiritual peripheral vision (Ephesians 5:1-20). You can perceive and understand the dangers around you, like temptations of lust, ego, and covetousness. Ask God to give you the wisdom to pay attention when He throws up the red flags (James 1:5-7). You will learn more about the Holy Spirit in chapter 5.

Be a listener. You always have access to God through prayer (Hebrews 4:16). He always hears you (John 11:41-42; 1 John 5:14-15). This is not one-way communication. Spend prayer time in silence so you can hear God through His Word, teachings, sermons, and life lessons. Listening to preaching is essential to faith-building (Romans 10:14-15; 15:4). You'll learn more about prayer in chapters 2 & 3.

Be a learner. Read the *road map*—the Bible (2 Timothy 2:15). It was written to guide you through every human situation (2 Timothy 3:14-17). It provides light (Psalm 119:105) and guides you on the right path (Psalm 119:9-16). Anyone who reads it without learning something isn't paying attention. You'll learn more about how to study the Bible in chapter 3.

Be a lover. The people you travel with are very important to the hike. Maintaining an atmosphere of love among the local church members is critical to our confidence in Jesus Christ (1 John 4:7-21). They provide safety, stability (Ecclesiastes 4:11-12), and encouragement through fellowship and mutual sharing of God's Word and the Holy Spirit (Hebrews 10:23-25). You'll learn more about being a part of a vibrant Christian community in chapters 4 & 9.

GETTING OTHERS TO HIKE WITH YOU

Recall a time you were afraid that God operated on a zero-tolerance policy?

_____

_____

If we received grace from God to join the hike, will He continue to show grace as you follow Him? (Heb. 4:16) How do you get this grace?

_____

_____

If Jesus died for all (John 3:16) and all can choose to confess (Romans 10:9) and those who choose to be Christ followers (Romans 10:13) have an invitation from God, do you believe you have the freedom to accept God and the freedom to not accept God to become a Christian? Explain:

_____

_____

Your hiking party is the people in the church of following Jesus Christ. The path you walk isn't very crowded. There is plenty of room for others to join. Who could you recruit for the trip to heaven?

Ask yourself: Who do I most want to protect from damage, danger, and dead ends? Your children and family are obvious candidates. You want your friends to avoid hell. Your neighbors are wandering in sin; and you're a good neighbor, aren't you? Why wouldn't you invite your co-workers to join you, since they are the people with whom you spend the most time? You could easily reason how much a person would have to hate someone heading to hell not to share Jesus with him or her.

You know Jesus now. He wants you to show others the way out of sin. Make a mental or written list of your family, friends, neighbors, and co-workers. Are they all following Jesus on His path? Have you ever told them about Jesus? Why not? Make a plan for sharing Jesus with at least five people on your list this year. Chapter 11 will help you begin to share with family and friends who should join you on your hike.

Road maps and GPS devices define your current location and give you direction to reach your destination or end goal. These tools warn about troublesome areas and keep you on the correct path. They provide a bird's eye view of what is ahead, and assist you in following the surest path during your journey. The Bible serves as your road map or GPS on the hike of your life, and it provides all of these benefits for reaching your destination along the surest route.

THE SOURCE

The Bible is *God-breathed*, which means that it was given in its original form by God to men through the Holy Spirit (2 Timothy 3:16-17). God led men to write the books of the Bible without dictating the text word-for-word but instead allowing their individual personalities to explain His thoughts and communicate His message. The Bible refers to itself as the *Word of God* to distinguish it as originating from God, and not originating from the will of man (2 Peter 1:20-21).

Christ-followers are to devote themselves to the private and public reading of Scripture, so that they can grow in their knowledge of Jesus Christ and their understanding of how to best follow Him (1 Timothy 4:13-15). What is amazing about this God-given road map is that it was penned by 40 different authors, contains 66 unique books or letters, and was written during a span of more than 1,500 years. Even with this variety of authors, a full library of unique books, and such a large time span, the Bible possesses a consistent theme and thread of God passionately pursuing people. From the writings of Moses—starting in Genesis—to the final prophets, the Old Testament (or Hebrew Scriptures) explained and foretold the truth of Jesus Christ (Luke 24:27). The Bible is your road map because it testifies or points you to Jesus (John 5:37-40). You should use this road map, the Bible, to examine what others are saying and to verify whether or not it is true (Acts 17:11).

Read the following verses in the Bible and put in your own words things learned from each Scripture.

2 Timothy 3:16–17

_____

2 Peter 1:20–21

_____

1 Timothy 4:13–15

_____

John 5:37–40

_____

The Bible is the only road map God has given you. It tells you how to go to heaven and to live in this world. The Scriptures tell you God's grand story from beginning to end and how you can play your part in God's great story. His story tells of the fall of humanity, the need for redemption, the solution of Jesus Christ, and the restoration of all things by the Holy Spirit.

God's Word is useful for teaching you about God, His character, His plan for humanity, and His willingness to make Himself known and available to anyone who will call upon Him (Romans 10:9-10). The Bible rebukes your sinful ways and refuses to leave you in them unchanged (2 Timothy 3:16-17). The Bible is first useful to *think* correctly, and then to *live* and *love* correctly. When you begin to understand God's unconditional love by grace through faith in Him, then His Spirit uses His Word to train you in righteousness (Titus 2:11-14; Ephesians 2:10).

THE EVIDENCE
History

The Bible is historically confirmed through other well-known leaders and discoveries of artifacts and ancient scrolls. Reputable historians outside of Scripture who lived shortly following the lives of the eyewitnesses of Jesus Christ compliment the content and accuracy of the Bible. Reputable ancient historians such as Polycarp, Ireneaus, Josephus, and many others all confirmed again and again in their own writings the life, death, and resurrection of Jesus Christ as well as the growth of followers of Jesus Christ after the resurrection even in the midst of great persecution and difficulty.

Archaeology

The Bible continues to be validated over and over again through the field of archaeology. There have been many questions about the Bible concerning its references to certain locations, landmarks, empires, and geography. While not all places or landmarks mentioned in the Bible have been found in recent history, archaeology continues to validate the Bible with each new discovery. Your road map continues to be trustworthy. For example, artifacts pertaining to people groups like the Hittites that are often spoken about in the Bible but rarely known about in historical findings have now been found in Turkey. Specific and detailed findings of locations and places like: the tower of Babel (Genesis 11), the city of Jericho (Joshua 1—8; Luke 19:1), the tomb of Joseph (Genesis 50), the city of Ninevah (Jonah 1), the pool of Gibeon (2 Samuel 2), the royal palace of Samaria (1 Kings 20), Solomon's horse stables called Meggido (1 Kings 9; 2 Chronicles 8), the royal palace where Esther was queen (Esther 1), the foundation of a synagogue where Jesus delivered a sermon (John 6), Jacob's well where Jesus spoke with the Samaritan woman (John 4), the house of Peter at Capernaum (Matthew 8), the Mount of Olives (2 Samuel 15), Herod's palace at Caesarea (Acts 23), and many other biblical sites can now be objectively verified. The world-wide flood (Genesis 6-9), the confusion of languages at the tower of Babel (Genesis 11), revolts and the tenure of kings, the fall of great ruling cities, and even Caiaphas of the New Testament (John 18), all possess external evidence which supports the overall redemptive history of the Bible.

Original Manuscripts

The current New Testament (or Greek Scriptures) is backed by thousands of preserved manuscripts, or copies of copies from which we compare and gain knowledge regarding the Scriptures. In their book, *Foundations: A Bible Study Guide*, Tom Holliday and Kay Warren remind us that: The Bible is translated from 24,000 copies of the New Testament alone and that there are more than 5,300 manuscripts to which one may refer and many are from the second or third century. No other ancient document can come even close in comparison to the reliability and authenticity of the Scriptures. When compared to other historically reliable documents like Homer's *Iliad* or Julius Caesar's *Gallic Wars*, the reliability of the Christ follower's road map is incomparable (*Beyond Belief to Convictions*, Josh McDowell, page 174) These manuscripts provide God's inspiration via eyewitness accounts, which help us understand the purpose and importance surrounding Jesus Christ (2 Peter 1:16-21).

Prophecy

The Bible is full of prophecies. From the beginning of the road map, in Genesis 3, you are promised that God will crush the head of Satan (Genesis 3:15). The virgin birth of Jesus (Isaiah 7:14), His being born in Bethlehem (Micah 5:1-2), His hailing from the tribe of Judah (Genesis 49:10), His being a descendent of King David (Jeremiah 23:5), and many more prophecies were all written in the Old Testament hundreds of years in advance of their fulfillment as recorded in the New Testament. Even the betrayal of Jesus (Psalm 41:9), the money paid for His betrayal (Zechariah 11:12-13), the way He would be mocked and spit upon (Isaiah 50:6), the response of Jesus during His accusation (Isaiah 53:7), His willingness to die a sinner's death (Isaiah 53:4-6), and His crucifixion (Zechariah 12:10), which predicted this method of execution before it officially existed, all point to a startling truth. Authors from a previous era unknowingly complemented the writings of authors from other future eras, and predicted events that hundreds of years later would become realities, thus verifying the inspiration of God. Seeing prophecies from early in the Old Testament fulfilled in the New Testament would be similar to seeing King Ferdinand II of Spain during the era of Christopher Columbus in the 15th century predicting the invasion of General Dwight Eisenhower on D-Day by naming the location, timing, and players involved.

Jesus recognized God as the Author of the Scriptures (Matthew 22:43-44), quoted the Bible

(Matthew 22:29), and called it the Word of God (Matthew 15:5-6; Mark 7:13). Jesus even confirmed the people and places of the Bible (Matthew 10:15; 12:40; 19:4-6; Luke 17:26) and predicted the New Testament church and its growth (Matthew 16:17-18), as well as His ongoing presence with Christ-followers who participate in this great mission of seeking and saving those who are lost (Matthew 28:16-20).

Former astronomy and mathematics professor Peter Stoner, author of *Science Speaks*, was once an unbelieving skeptic who tried to test the Bible's prophetic accuracy. During his observation, he studied the probability of accuracy relating to the 48 major Old Testament prophecies concerning the coming of Jesus Christ as the Messiah. He concluded that a person would have only a 1 in 10^{17} chance to fulfill and live out just eight of the prophecies. And the chance that any one man could fulfill all 48 major prophecies would be an insurmountable 1 in 10^{157}. In fact, these odds are so high it has once been said that you could stack quarters a foot deep and cover the whole state of Texas, while marking only one of those quarters with a black X. The odds that you could then travel the whole state of Texas blindfolded and only pick one quarter out of that stack and successfully select the one with the black "X" is about the same odds as one person being able to fulfill all 48 prophecies (Stoner, *Science Speaks, Moody Press Chicago 1944, Online Edition*).

Orienteering

The best way to understand and follow the map is to read and know the Bible. When you take time to read it daily, you allow the Holy Spirit to speak to your conscience about what God the Father desires to say to you. Experienced hikers desire to study the road ahead, rate their progress, and follow the right path. When you read the Bible, it gives wisdom for your journey.

Read Daily!

For every hiker, knowing and understanding the road map is invaluable. Every time you read God's Word, it enables you to understand more about who God is, what He has done, and His good and perfect will for your life. If you need to purchase a Bible, ask your pastor, discipleship leader, or Bible study teacher how to select one. Find a good place to read your Bible and spend time in prayer asking God's Spirit within you to help you understand it. You can begin reading the New Testament by starting in the book of Mark or John, or you can follow any of the other reading plans suggested in the appendix. Ultimately, the Bible guides you to become the person God created you to be (2 Timothy 3:15). Again, each time you read, ask God in prayer to make it understandable. Make Bible reading a part of your routine each day.

Study Regularly!

Studying the Bible for godly understanding is a worthy pursuit. When you were in school, you studied not only to pass the test, but also to gain knowledge for life. Gaining knowledge for living results from being in the Word a little deeper than just daily skimming or reading affords (2 Timothy 2:15). It requires diligent study. As a follower of Jesus Christ, you study in order to know what is right, how to endure hardship, and how to be prepared for whatever life tosses at you (2 Timothy 4:1-8). The next chapter teaches you how to study God's Word. The Bible shows God's story of His desired relationship with humanity while Satan tries to disrupt at every turn.

Memorize Consistently!

In Deuteronomy 6:1-7, we get the heartbeat of God as He desires you to know Him by studying His Word and teaching your kids to do the same. You cannot share what you do not own. You start by committing key verses to memory so that when you need an answer, the Holy Spirit will bring it to your attention to apply in any immediate situation. When Jesus was tempted by the devil after fasting 40 days, He continually responded by faithfully quoting Scripture (Matthew 4:1-11). When you begin to memorize Scripture, you will realize a transformation of how you think because you will begin to think in the way God desires (Romans 12:2). Since belief determines behavior, it is an important spiritual discipline to set your mind on wholesome things.

Consistently memorizing God's Word allows you to be made new in the attitude of your mind, as you become a new creation (Ephesians 4:23-24). Every time you memorize Scripture, you actually follow the example of Jesus—He was constantly quoting the Old Testament.

Usually the discipline of Scripture memory just starts with one verse at a time. There are many methods of memorization, and you must find one that works for you. Repetition brings great success. You may write verses on note cards and leave them in a prominent spot. While you're stuck in traffic, waiting on an appointment, or maybe before you go to bed, read it and reread it trying to soak the Scripture into your memory. When you make an index card for a new verse, try to go back and review the previous ones you have made. You may use your computer, phone, or tablet to read and memorize verses. Singing Scripture speeds the process of memorization and increases retention. Search for professionally produced songs of Scripture memory. No matter the method of memorization, the discipline of memorization enables you to think biblically as you strive toward understanding correct doctrine, overcoming temptation in your new life in Jesus, and impressing His Word on your heart. Some verses to consider memorizing would be as follows:

Deuteronomy 6:4–9	*John 3:16*
Psalm 1	*Acts 1:7–8*
Psalm 23	*Ephesians 2:3–10*
Psalm 73:26	*1 Timothy 1:15–17*
Psalm 139	*Hebrews 11:1*
Proverbs 23:19	*1 John 1:9*
Proverbs 3:5,6	*1 John 5:13*
Matthew 6:21	

The best way to memorize Scripture is through repetition and review. This may seem basic, but what you are essentially doing is allowing the passage to *live* with you, and while doing so, you are also meditating on it. Action begins with a thought, and if you want your actions to reflect and exude Jesus, your thoughts must be with and on Him. Memorizing Scripture on a regular basis can transform your first reaction to circumstances into a biblical response.

Your Scripture memorization focus should be determined by the unique work God is doing in your heart. Select verses that cause you to pause when you read over them. Don't try to mechanically memorize verses from a list you find online. You want to memorize Scripture that aids you in defeating the devil in a moment of weakness, and your weaknesses are very specific to you.

Apply Immediately!

As you can see, the Bible, your map for direction in life, is more than a history book or a storybook.

It is your guide for life decisions. The goals of daily reading, regularly studying, and consistently memorizing are to give us wisdom for everyday living when we apply it or live out the principles it teaches. You can begin to live it out immediately.

Read Colossians 3:2 and Philippians 4:8 and write down some areas on which God wants you to focus.

Colossians 3:2

_____

_____

Philippians 4:8

_____

_____

What is the difference between simply reading and applying what you read?

_____

Deuteronomy 6:1-14 teaches us to do what with God's Word?

_____

_____

You will begin to see changes in your life as you follow and live what you read from the Bible. It truly is life changing. Every time you are in the Word of God, ask: How does God want me to apply and respond to what I've read in His Word?

The Conversation

Every time you read God's Word, make sure to ask God to illuminate His Word by His Spirit in your life. As you read and study, pray about the truths you learn and for the courage you need. Ask God to help you understand His love, to embrace His grace, and grow in belief each and every day.

Is the concept of prayer mysterious to you? Prayer or meditation is a foundational element of nearly every world religion. However, Jesus uniquely sets Christian prayer apart in its character, tone, and content. In Matthew 6:5-15, He describes prayer as simply a conversation between you and your Father God. Jesus denounces praying out of a motivation of being heard by other people around you, or using certain cliché or mantra-like stanzas in hopes of moving a deity. He casts all of these motivations aside and welcomes you to talk to your Father God in the language and respectful, but not fearful, tone you would use in addressing your own earthly father. Your Father God, Jesus reminds you, already knows what you need before you even ask for it.

Questions that may surface in your mind include: Why should I request anything from a God who is unchanging? Why should I petition a God whose plans are already sovereignly set? The answer is that God sovereignly chooses to work through the requests of His children, and Jesus implores His followers to take their requests, petitions, fears, and desires to their Father God regularly. God has chosen to work through your choice to pray to Him.

A second set of questions you may ask: Why would God listen to me? How can an infinite God hear someone as finite as me? When you ask these questions, you have properly understood your place in God's universe. You have recognized your insignificance combined with your unworthiness to approach the pure holiness of your Almighty God. Do not ever relinquish your correct understanding of your self in light of His majesty. However, the complete answer to your question resides in the glory of the crucified and then risen Jesus who purchased you through His blood and now provides unlimited access to the very throne room of the universe. Through the adoption you have received via the death of Jesus in your place, you are now a child of the King. He welcomes you into His presence (Hebrews 10:19-22).

Jesus' example prayer in Matthew 6:9-13 was offered to the disciples as an instructional aid when they asked how to pray (Luke 11:1). Jesus did not intend this prayer to be quoted word-for-word (remember his denouncing of repetitive mantras?), but to be used as an example for content, attitude, and tone. As stated earlier, prayer should resemble a conversation with your heavenly dad, though from the perspective of reverence and awe in light of God's sacred holiness (Matthew 6:9). Prayer should flow from a heart that groans for the redemption of all things and the completion of God's ultimate redemptive will in the lives of those for whom you pray, your own life, and the world at large. Prayer is not intended to sound like a petty wish list of personal ambition, but more a cry from a child for the good, kind intention of a loving father to be carried out. If you believe that God is good and that He is all-powerful, you will yearn for His good will to be experienced in your world (Matthew 6:10). It is from this perspective that requests are to be made for daily provision, continuous forgiveness, and ongoing protection (Matthew 6:11-13).

Although you are not limited to pray in any particular geographical location, physical posture, or time of day, Jesus would many times spend time in prayer alone, both in the morning and the evening, perhaps because it was when He could most easily escape the distractions of others. He prayed through the night before selecting His disciples and before facing His crucifixion (Matthew 26:36-46; Mark 1:35-37; 6:45-46; Luke 5:16; 6:12-16). After Jesus resurrected, His disciples regularly met together for extended times of corporate prayer, which led to demonstrations of Gospel power or confident decision-making (Acts 4:31; 13:1-3; 14:21-23; 16:25-30). Both private and corporate prayer are marks of a vibrant, humble Christ-follower.

Specific prayer requests should be offered to God regularly, not in a rote, repetitive way similar to incantations, but out of a heart of persistent faith in His ability to accomplish all things. For example, the Apostle Paul's attitude represented a call to ongoing, persistent cries of Christ-followers for God to open clear pathways for the Gospel to break through to unreached people (Ephesians 6:18-20). Yet Paul also acknowledged that a request should cease once it is clear that the request is in direct conflict with God's intended goals (2 Corinthians 12:7-10).

Matthew 6:11–13 teaches you to pray for certain areas of your life. Name the ones you see in Christ's model prayer.

_____

_____

Take time now to list a few prayer requests and begin praying for them daily.

_____

_____

Your prayer time can be greatly enhanced by studying the prayers of believers throughout Scripture. You will find prayers related to confession of personal or national sin (Psalm 51; Ezra 9:5-15; Daniel 9:3-19), thanksgiving and praise (Psalm 118; 1 Samuel 2:1-10; Colossians 4:2-4), intercession for the well-being of others (Exodus 33:12-18; Ephesians 3:14-19; 1 Timothy 2:1-2), and simple requests or petitions (1 Samuel 1:9-18; James 5:14-20). Also present in Scripture are prayers of imprecation, which request God's righteous judgment against enemies (Psalm 59). Although you may find this type of prayer foreign to your current understanding of God, imprecatory prayers stem from a righteous heart which views evil through God's eyes, and cries out to Him for holy justice. Ultimately, these prayers decry injustice, and place unjust situations in God's hands instead of seeking personal vengeance (Revelation 6:9-11).

Outfitted with your road map, the Bible, you can trust in its reliability, remain oriented on Jesus' path through regular study, and communicate with your Guide via prayer. These are the essentials of every Christ-follower. Keep them by your side, and you'll never need to be concerned about being lost again.

chapter 3

Your Road Map →
part 2

Tommy Swindol

THE ASCENT INTO BIBLE STUDY

Most Christ-followers know reading God's Word is important. The Bible is God's message to all believers and He expects you, as one of His children, will want to hear His message and examine it. However, for many different reasons, most Christ-followers find this an intimidating charge. It may appear a daunting mountain they fear incapable of climbing. The Bible appears so vast; you may not understand how it is organized, its language, or its terminology. It can be challenging; many Christ-followers just give up and never read the Bible, or have never read it through entirely.

With a rise in biblical illiteracy, it is ever important for you not only to *read* the Bible, but also to dig in and **study** the depths and riches that lie within its pages. It's important to get the big picture of the Bible and see how you fit in its story. Once that begins to happen, you will think about the Bible differently. You will begin to see the beauty and flow of the greater story of creation, fall, redemption, and restoration.

After all, the Bible is no ordinary book. It's a collection of books written by different authors in several languages over a period of almost 2,000 years. It's a library whose books are shelved by type and topic: history, the Law, the Prophets, poems and wisdom literature, eyewitness accounts of Jesus (the Gospels), collections of letters, and mind-blowing apocalyptic descriptions of the past, present, and future. It is, by far, the most incredible book ever written.

Bernard Ramm, famous theologian and apologist, said, "No other book has been so chopped, knifed, sifted, scrutinized, and vilified. What book has been subject to such a mass attack as the Bible? With such venom and skepticism? With such thoroughness and erudition? Upon every chapter, line, and tenet? A thousand times over, the death knell of the Bible has been sounded, the funeral procession formed, the inscription cut on the tombstone, and committal read. But somehow, the corpse never stays put!"[1]

This is a journey of discovery. Just as the disciples didn't just "get it" or understand it from the beginning, but instead, progressed through a process of discovery, you will require the same. You can't expect to open the Bible and just "get it" either; you've got to be willing to progress through the process as well. You've got to be willing to misunderstand at times, and not to understand at all in others, so that you can grow in an overall understanding. The Bible is your map or GPS so you cannot simply ignore it; if you do, you will get nowhere.

OUR TRAILHEAD: PROPER PERSPECTIVE

The way to begin your Bible study journey is to develop a proper perspective of what it means to actually *study* the Bible. It involves expectation for what God has for you, openness to the Scriptures, and a reverence to these being the very words of the Most High. Perspective will become your trailhead. It's where your journey truly begins.

What kind of outlook should you have on the Bible? How do you view study time?

_____

_____

Expectation: The Wonders of the Scriptures

As you study the Bible, you'll be amazed at its riches. Author Bob Grahmann expressed this truth when he stated: "From dizzying heights of grandeur to the depths of despair and back, you'll emerge convinced that the Bible is the best library you've ever read!"[2] You should possess a high-level expectation mixed with prayer when you approach the Bible.

Openness: Ready to Be Changed

Having the proper perspective implies coming to the Bible not only with a sense of openness, but also with incredible expectation. You open the Bible ready for it to *change* you. Come to the Bible thinking you will find something vastly wiser, more piercing, and more worldview shaping than any of the opinions or contemporary ideas you come across in your lifetime. You will discover that this is truly the very Word of God and should be approached with the venerable thought and prayer that God is speaking directly to you, not simply to inform you, but to bring about change in you. Pray for God to open your eyes to who you really are and to who you could really become in Christ.

Reverence: A Respect for Life-Changing Words

The last perspective with which to approach God's Word is a sense of reverence or esteem. You recognize your true need for God and you *expect* the Bible to meet that need by convicting you of your sin, bringing you to a point of repentance and forgiveness, and ultimately providing hope.

Second Timothy 3:16 explains how all of Scripture is God-breathed and is helpful in teaching, rebuking, correcting, and for training in righteousness. All of the Bible is useful and worthy of your time—yes, even the genealogies and the odd and unusual Old Testament feasts. It's all inspired directly from your Creator, and helps you to be sufficient in sound doctrine and day-to-day life. There is nothing that God expects of you that He does not provide in His Word. He helps you understand what to do and gives you the motivation to do it.

For example, Philippians 2:12-13 discusses how you should work out your salvation with fear and trembling because it is God who works on your **will** and **actions** according to His purpose. That means it's not you but God who will give you the power to live the way you should and even have the will to do it. It's on Him, not you. Without coming to the Bible with reverence and respect toward wonders like that, you could pass right over such life-changing truths!

2 Timothy 3:16 described the Bible/Scripture as what?

_____

Read Psalm 119:105. According to this verse, how does the Word of God/Bible help you on your journey?

_____

USING THE MAP

Bible study should impact your mind, heart, and attitude. It's not just about accumulating *knowledge.* God prepares people to see things in His Word in unique ways, and there are some people who will see things and think on things that you've never seen or thought about. Therefore, God doesn't want you to just open the Bible, shut your eyes, and point your finger, taking that to be God's direction for your life that day. God's desire is for you to study His Word methodically. He wants you to read it over time so that you begin to understand it, and the more you do, the more you understand about yourself. God has chosen the method to reveal Himself—through written language, and any written message requires studying the meaning to fully grasp what is being said. To stay on the trail in unfamiliar territory, you have to know how to use the map. In learning how to use the map, it is helpful to know how it is put together as shown in Appendix A and C.

Context: How Does the Passage Fit?

Grasping God's intention for each part of the Bible requires you to read it in *context.* That means you understand the **literary** context, which includes the grammar of the day and identifying what type of literature it is (prose, poetry, etc). Is the passage you're reading a letter to specific people? Is it a parable (a fictional story told to communicate a truth)? As with any book, literary context helps you dive into the language and expectations of the writer. After all, you do this subconsciously every time you open up a fiction or nonfiction book or read a blog, or poem. You should train yourself to use the same approach with the Bible, bringing yourself into the original context of the passage.

You should consider the **cultural** context of the Scripture. This includes the social, geographical, and political factors that are relevant to the author's backdrop. This is where a study Bible or Bible handbook really becomes helpful. Several helpful, and even free, commentaries can be found in Appendix B.

The **theological** context becomes incredibly important to discover. Every single passage in the Bible fits into the overall picture of God's Word; therefore, set out to grasp the broader context of each passage compared to the entire Bible. Don't just read different texts or verses in isolation of each other; instead, read them in the broader context of the whole chapter, the whole book, and the whole Bible so that you don't sacrifice the actual meaning of a passage for a shortcut understanding of a singular verse. As David Platt states, "The Bible communicates eternal content through specific contexts."[3] You need to know those specific contexts.

Observation: What Does the Passage Say?

Start by reading passages of the Bible with no commentary help. Read the passage several times. This will help you discover and interpret the Scriptures on your own without the help of an "expert." This will make your time with the Lord and application of the passage all the more beneficial. Set out to read the Bible **broadly**, but study it **deeply**.

Reading broadly is a good way to get an overview. When you decide to plunge into a portion more thoroughly, use an inductive approach to the passage, meaning let the text *speak*, and this will help you gain depth of insight toward the passage. Inductive study is just reading the passage without preconceived notions or assumptions, but simply unpacking the words, sentences, and paragraphs. During this observation stage, you will want to spend some time, even days, reading through the entire book of the Bible (for example if you are trying to understand James chapter two, then read the whole book of James several times). Read through it completely more than once. Look for *themes* that may be woven in the chapters. Take notes on the ideas and subjects that jump out at you. Again, don't incorporate study tools yet; you want to wrestle with the passage of Scripture instead of just relying on what a commentator thinks. This gives an opportunity for God's Word to speak personally to you in a unique way.

After reading through the entire book several times, try to slow down and read the book verse-by-verse. This may seem tedious, but remember that you are not just reading the Bible. You are *discovering* it. You are treating it as though it is a great treasure that your life depends upon—because it is.

Because God's Word is truly alive, you can study the same passage several times and continue to discover new, relevant truths throughout a lifetime of study. It's incredible and can only be discovered through verse-by-verse inductive study. Be *patient* as you read the verses. Don't skim, but look at everything as you listen to what the Lord is saying. Bring every question you have to the passage: Who wrote this? What's the author saying? When and where did all this take place? Why is this passage included in the Bible?

Read your passage over and over, including what comes just before and just after the passage.

Notice the subjects or topics on which the author spends time in the book. Start your observations with big picture study, and then zoom in to each individual verse.

Understanding: What's the Point of the Passage?

This is where the theological question, "What does it mean?" comes into play. Why would God place this text or verse in the Bible? You shouldn't forget that Scripture was God's Word to other people before it ever became God's Word to current-day Christ followers so you need to understand the timeless principles within the Scripture. You will begin to understand the point when you discover access trails on our journey by using cross-referencing. After all, the best interpreter of Scripture is Scripture. So when you're struggling to understand, let other parts of the Bible help you understand.

Application: Why Does This Passage Matter?

Bible study always ends with application; it focuses on *action*. There is a single point to a passage but there are many applications found within it. Applying the passage to your life involves asking the questions: What is God teaching me? What am I sharing with my family? *Why does this matter to my life?* In answering this last question, you must recognize the distinction between the original audience and you (their living under the Law and your living under grace, or their living in the nation of Israel versus your living in this country). Then, set out to find the similarities between the original audience and yourself (you're both the Church; you have similar struggles and human relationships; you serve the same God and demonstrate the same faith). Don't ask: How does this relate to me? Ask: How does this *apply* to my marriage, my family, my church, my city, and my situation?

When studying the Bible, you shouldn't get accustomed to accepting a blurred, vague treatment of Scripture, but instead should expect clear, specific, life-changing application for *today*. In doing that, there are four important benchmark questions to ask based on the passage you are studying:

#1 Who should I be? How does my character need to change?

#2 What should I think? How does this text change the way I look at life?

#3 What do I do? Don't just read the Word; obey it.

#4 Where should I go? The passage should move you to go out and share the Gospel.

Keep in mind that these four benchmark questions are in place to help *guide* your thoughts toward practical application. Don't just study God's Word for the sake of studying or to feel better about yourself. Put the Word into *practice*. Jesus accentuates this in Luke 11:28 when He explains that those who not only hear the Word of God, but also *put it into practice* are blessed by Him.

You must draw application to real problems in the *thick* of navigating rough terrain in your life. Much of the Bible is written from and addresses times of distress as well as delight. Therefore, the hard question is: How do I get real life answers? When you are completely lost and life is beating you up, how do you find answers from the Scriptures? You will find your answers through application.

Finally, a thought-provoking and incredible truth in finding the summit of Bible study is grasping the fact that it all comes back to Jesus. Think about that. *All* of Scripture leads us to Christ. In fact, making this connection is the difference between *reading* the Bible and *studying* the Bible. Martin Luther said that the Bible is the "cradle of Christ," which means all biblical history and prophecy ultimately points to Jesus. Studying the Bible through that lens provides an overarching story of what God has done for you *through* Jesus and how to fully apply the truth found within the Scriptures. An example of how to walk through this study process is found in Appendix C.

Read Hebrews 4:12. According to this verse, How does God's Word, the Bible, help you on your journey?

_____

_____

Read Luke 11:28 and 2 Timothy 3:16. How is the Bible different from other books you read?

_____

_____

IV. ORIENTEERING: DEVELOPING A ROUTINE

As noted in the previous chapter, orienteering involves using a map, compass, detailed strategies, and navigational skills to move along an unfamiliar path to reach your destination. Biblical orienteering means that you will walk with God through the day, reminding yourself of what you learned in the Scriptures. To do this, just as in orienteering, it's going to take prayerful strategy in determining what your Bible study routine will look like and how to adjust it to your lifestyle and personality.

Find a Place

Once you have found your place to study the Bible, you have passed the first major obstruction, because finding the right place is key to your success. If you try to spend quality time studying the Bible while lying in bed just before you go to sleep after a long day, failure is inevitable. Decide to have a specific place for your study time with God—a place that's comfortable with good lighting. Be as consistent as possible with this place, maybe even creating a station there with all of your "tools": Bible, pen, journal, reading plan, commentaries, and so forth so that when you go there, you're able to simply go to your place and everything is ready.

Choose a Time

Work to build into your life a regular encounter with studying God's Word, personally and quietly meditating on the Scriptures without being rushed. The pace of our culture is maddening and you must learn how to do this in "the thick of traffic," but you'll find this time to be the most beneficial time of your day.

Even if you are not a morning person, the early morning is a good choice because it sets the spiritual tone for the whole day, and is the least likely time of day for an interruption. You seldom receive a call from a friend or client at 6:00 a.m. *Early morning* means before your schedule opens up to the rest of the world. Every day has a time frame where people expect you to answer your phone, send the e-mail, show up for work, or whatever. So before all of that happens, set aside a chunk of time to study the Word and gain insight for your day.

If the morning doesn't work, then plan for the midday or evening. Maybe a lunch break fits better into your schedule or just after putting the kids to bed. Regardless of *when* you make it, make sure it's planned and is just as sternly held as an appointment with your boss or date night with your wife. This is an opportunity to commune with the living God. It will be the most important and beneficial meeting of every day! If you view your time spent alone with God as an appointment to be kept in your daily calendar, you will be less apt to miss or skip it.

There is no *right* or *wrong* time of day. Whatever time of day you choose, let it be the best time of day for you when your mind is alert and ready to focus on God's message to you.

Use the Right Tools

Begin by obtaining a whole Bible (not just a New Testament) in a version you are comfortable reading. Readability is key, and you should talk with your pastor about which one may be right for you. Regardless of what version you pick, make sure it is accurately translated. If you use more than one translation, it's a wonderful idea to have a Bible for your primary use while also having additional translations nearby to see how each varies in structure and wording as you read in context repeatedly as previously discussed. The best type of Bible to get is a study Bible because it includes a simple, brief outline of the Bible, brief introductions to each book of the Bible, maps, and various resources helpful to your study.

To get the most out of studying the Bible, consider choosing the right tools to aid you in learning, such as a Bible dictionary, commentary, concordance, or lexicon. This doesn't mean you need to spend a lot of money on obtaining these tools. Many of them are free to you online. Such a list of specific resources can be found in Appendix B.

Choose a Bible Reading Plan or Bible Study

It's going to take some persistence to develop the habit of studying Scripture. You might want to use a Bible reading plan similar to the ones provided at www.YouVersion.com (a free website that provides various plans for reading through the whole Bible in a certain amount of time, topical studies, *First Steps* reading plans, etc.), or you may want to read as described below. No matter how you study the Word, constantly ask questions: What do I see here? What should I learn? What is God telling me to do?

This will aid in having a more *focused* time of studying. As you dig deeper, you can return to your questions with the answers you discover. If you just pick up your Bible and start reading randomly each day, you may have a difficult time understanding what you read, or applying it to your daily life.

If you're digging into God's Word for the first time, start with the Gospel of Mark, and then go on to John. Why? The book of Mark is quick and fast-paced, while John focuses on the things Jesus claimed about Himself. Mark tells about what Jesus *did*, while John tells about what Jesus *said*. John has some of the simplest and clearest passages, such as John 3:16, which discuses the simplicity of salvation but also some of the deepest and most profound passages, such as John 1:1-18, which discuses the doctrine of the Trinity and the mysterious work of Jesus while on earth.

Once you've studied through John, simply go on to the next book, Acts. This is Luke's sequel to his account of Jesus, picking up the account at the point of His ascension. In this action-packed letter, you will learn how the early church began and how the Gospel spread throughout the entire Roman Empire. Understanding the letters of Paul, Peter, and others that follow in the Bible will be much easier once you've read Acts.

Next, move on to Romans. This letter is completely different as it introduces the writing of the apostle Paul and general Christian faith. In Romans, Paul describes the basic philosophy of the Christian faith, centering everything on God's grace.

Once you've taken your time and studied through these books, jump into some of the narrative stories of the Old Testament. Genesis and Exodus are good places to begin, while possibly including the Psalms at the same time. Consider reading one psalm each day as a preface to the day's study in Genesis or Exodus. Once you've come this far, you will have read one book from every "shelf" in the Bible's library: the Gospels, the Law, Old Testament history, the Epistles, New Testament history, and the wisdom literature.

As a side note, while you're developing Bible study habits, find a friend or join in with a group of people who are also interested in studying the Bible. Find a Bible study that is serious about digging into the Scriptures. Most of the Bible was written to communities of people and is therefore best studied in *community* with other Christ-followers. For this reason, getting plugged into a Bible study group or Sunday School class in addition to regularly attending a church service is essential in forming accountability for a growing relationship in Christ.

Pray

One of the most common reasons why Christ-followers don't study the Bible is: "I just don't understand it!" As noted in the previous chapter, you cannot under value the power and effectiveness of prayer.

Pray Psalm 119:18 each time you read the Bible: the essence of your prayer should be: "Lord, open my eyes so that I can observe the deep wonders in Your Word." As the prayer of the psalmist illustrates, there are wonders throughout "the law" or the Word of God, and it is your desire for God to reveal them to you. The Bible contains the most magnificent, breathtaking instructions of God. And, just like the psalmist, you need to be aware that most people don't often feel or see wonderful things as wonderful. So David asks to see. You need to begin by doing the same. When you go to the Word, you are asking specifically to see with spiritual eyes what is so wonderful. Don't think it doesn't matter that you read extraordinary things without recognizing them as extraordinary. It matters, and therefore you need to come with expectation to study the Bible so the Lord can and *will* open your eyes to the wonders of His Word.

Praying is talking to the Guide who drew the map and who knows its every detail. Prayer is simply two-way communication between you and God. When you study the Bible, you will always need God's revealing power to grasp what He's trying to show you. The Bible, because of its spiritual nature, is not just any ordinary book. You are going to need Divine aid as you study it to be able to fully understand what you are reading. Always read the Bible expecting God to speak to you through the power of the Holy Spirit. Some Christ followers don't realize prayer includes listening. Instead of constantly talking and petitioning the Lord, give Him time to speak to you in His still small voice (1 Kings 19:12). He will teach you how to apply His words to your life. He will encourage you and give you daily direction if you take it to heart. If you get stuck in a rut, maybe the plan you've chosen is not right for you or you simply need a change. Change it up until you find the perfect fit.

Meditate on the Word

After studying the Bible, spend time meditating on it. This involves prayer. It involves talking to God, listening to Him, telling Him about your struggles and concerns, and then listening for His guidance in your spirit. God's guidance comes from thinking about biblical principles that give you discernment in the answers to life's problems, challenges, and questions. Meditation requires prayer as you recall the verses read throughout the day. Continuing to think and dwell on the meaning of what you read will allow it to grow and produce deeper understanding. You cannot just read about algebra and immediately grasp it. You must work through it with plenty of practice. When reading and meditating on the Bible, you are cultivating your understanding.

Meditation involves worshiping the Lord and giving Him praise for the truths found in Scripture. So let your response to Bible study include this. First Peter 2:9 states that you are part of a chosen people and a royal priesthood, and it goes a step further by proclaiming you to be God's special possession who has the privilege to **declare His praises** because He has called you out of darkness and into the light.

Move beyond a checklist approach and actually *meditate* or mentally chew on the Word. Psalm 1:2 says you are blessed when you delight in the Lord's instruction and when you think about it day and night. This is the very definition of meditating. You will be blessed through this opportunity to think deeply and reflect on God's ways.

Memorize Scripture

If you're curious about *how* you can begin to memorize Scripture, start by setting aside time and praying for discipline. As you set aside a window of time in the day to study the Bible, spend at least 5 or 10 minutes of your study time memorizing Scripture. If you decide to memorize Scripture for 5 or 10 minutes a day, you can hide an incredible amount of Scripture in your heart! See previous chapter for more ways to memorize Scripture.

Journal

Many Christ-followers find that journaling helps them stay on track during their study time. So as you read your Bible, perhaps keep a notebook or pad of paper and a pen at your side. Write down anything that seems important to you. Don't be afraid to write in your Bible. If there is a verse that stands out, underline it or highlight it. You may even want to make a brief note in the margin of your Bible beside the verse. In your notebook, journal your thoughts on the passage, what comes to mind when applying it to your life, and things that you want to begin praying over. You will find that this will begin to be a valuable record of your life. Later, you will be amazed and encouraged when you go back and see the evidence of answered prayers and wise decisions in your life.

Conclusion

Bible study is a skill that is important for every Christ-follower to develop. Remember that learning how to study the Bible is a process. You will get better at it the more you do it, but it may be a little rocky at first.

Ascending into life-changing Bible study begins at the trailhead of proper perspective—expecting God to reveal His wonders through Scripture, opening your heart and mind to its concepts, respecting the God who inspired them, and trusting Him to be your Guide. When studying the Bible, you need to set out to understand the full context: literary, cultural, and theological, while observing what the passage says, understanding the point, and applying what it is telling you. And finally, orient your life around Bible study by finding a place and time, surrounding yourself with helpful study tools, and deeply involving prayer, Scripture memory, deep thinking, worship, and journaling. All of this may sound daunting but start step-by-step and you will find it refreshing. Doing these things will begin a lifelong journey of incredible, pointed, Spirit-filled Bible study.

Bishop Pollock once said, "The Bible is a corridor between two eternities down which walks the Christ of God; His invisible steps echo through the Old Testament, but we meet Him face to face in the throne room of the New; and it is through that Christ alone, crucified for me, that I have found forgiveness for sins and life eternal. The Old Testament is summed up in the word Christ; the New Testament is summed up in the word Jesus; and the summary of the whole Bible is that Jesus is the Christ." Let your life be summed up with the same truth, and may it begin with your decision to take the journey of Spirit-led Bible study. May it change not only you, but also the eternity of many.

This is a journey of discovery. As noted earlier, the first disciples did not immediately "get it," and neither will you. It's a **process** of disciplined discovery. At times the terrain will be steep and jagged; it will take great effort to make the journey of truly studying the Bible and understanding it. The further you climb on your hike, the stronger and more blessed you will be. The more effort you put into it, the more strength you will gain. So study the Bible well, and set out on the expedition of a lifetime.

What time of the day are you going to set aside as a regular appointment to read and study God's Word?

_____

What reading plan are you going to use? Where in the Bible are you going to begin reading? (See Appendix E and www.YouVersion.com)

_____

3. What verse do you plan to memorize first? Write it out here.

_____

_____

_____

End Notes

[1]Ramm, Bernard. *Protestant Christian Evidences.* (Chicago: Moody Press, 1967), 112.
[2]Grahmann, Bob. *Transforming Bible Study: Understanding God's Word Like You've Never Read It Before* (Downers Grove: Intervarsity Press, 2003), 12.
[3]Platt, David. *How to Study the Bible Part 1.* (http://www.brookhills.org/media/schurch/ secret church how to study the bible/)

Your Road Map Part 2

Your Outfitter

THE CHURCH

As a new Christ-follower, one of the most important decisions you make early on this path is to find and get involved in a local church to help you on your journey. This chapter introduces you to the value and benefit of being a part of a local church.

What may be common for one person may be questioned by another. Some people are part of a church because their parents and grandparents were a part. In fact, for them, church is a fundamental part of life. But for many others, church is something very new and unfamiliar.

WHAT IS *CHURCH*?

Many people point to a building with a steeple and claim that structure to be the church. While the architectural structure may look pleasing, Jesus calls His *followers* the church, not a piece of real estate. Only *people* can be the church as described in the Bible. When you are part of a church, you are not part of an address, but rather you are part of a vibrant, diverse community of people all seeking to follow Jesus.

It is a blessing to be a part of a spiritual organism that is so different, yet so alike. The family of God is unique. The <u>universal</u> church consists of all who have placed faith in Jesus as the One who paid our sin debt and saved us by His grace. The *local* church is made up of believers who agree on basic Bible doctrines and desire to worship with others that believe as they do. They are people who show and shower their love towards others (John 13:34-35).

The Lord has graciously extended the gift of salvation to you and placed you in His family. It is important to see the *universal* church of our Lord includes *every* person that has been born into His family (Ephesians 2:8-10). Some believers at other *local* extensions of the Lord's church may not think or believe exactly like you do, but that does not mean they are not Christians! The poor and rich, all ethnicities and heritages, and all ages and types of people who become Christ-followers are one in Jesus. All of these brothers and sisters have the welcome privilege and stated purpose of Jesus as Reconciler to come together to learn and worship at a local church (Ephesians 2:11–18).

We all have one thing in common: our faith in the saving grace of the Lord Jesus Christ! This makes you part of His great big church family and also gives you an opportunity to be part of a local church congregation that is helping you grow in Him!

WHY SHOULD I ATTEND A LOCAL CHURCH?

If the Bible is our guide and map for our journey, then you should see what it says about relationships with other Christ-followers.

Meeting together makes you stronger.

You come together for advice, encouragement, and exhortation. You also need to hear the Word of God. A great way to accomplish this is by the preaching and teaching found in church. We prepare for potential problems in life. The more prepared we are, the more easily we can face challenges. At church we hear lessons taught with practical applications given for daily living. Ephesians 6:10-18 tells us that we can be outfitted to face great difficulties. Most of this preparation comes from sitting under the teaching and preaching of the Word combined with your daily reading of it. When you have good Bible teachers, you learn life lessons by seeing Scripture applied to everyday experiences. Preaching and teaching from the Word helps you become what God intends you to be by building spiritual character in your life.

We are to praise God. Psalm 22:22 indicates that while you can praise God alone, you should also do so among other Christ-followers. Psalm 134:2 reinforces this concept. Because you have a wonderful God, you want to respond to His mercy and grace by corporately praising Him.

Early in the Bible, God established six days for us to work. He set aside one day out of seven to take time to recognize Him by praising Him and giving thanks for His blessings. We accomplish this recognition in our local church as a community of redeemed people from all walks of life.

We can grow friendships that become a source of encouragement and help. Ecclesiastes 4:9–12 indicates the strength others provide to that which we cannot accomplish alone. First John 1:7 and 1 John 2:9-10 show the love and dependence we need in good relationships with other Christ followers. At church you meet people going through similar phases of life; however, each is mutually desiring to face life's challenges uniquely according to God's Word. We will find friends with kids similar in age to our own and shared wisdom among parents becomes most welcomed. You may find a closeness in friendships with people at church in ways you never expected or experienced. The Lord teaches you the value of others in 1 Corinthians 12 and how you are to help others. The apostle Paul said (Galatians 6:2) you are to help others struggling and share in their heavy load.

After reading the section above entitled "What is the church?'

_____

_____

Describe the difference in the "universal church" and the "local church."

_____

_____

Read Hebrews 10:25 and Romans 10:17. List reasons and the result of hearing God's Word together.

_____

_____

Ecclesiastes 4:9-12, I John 1:7, I John 2:9-10 all show value in attending church with others. Why?

_____

_____

WHY WE ARE NOT ALL ALIKE

Churches are like many other organizations—they are filled with different types of people! The demographics of most classes and congregations are vastly different. Some are more educated than others. Some may be from larger families than others. Some are young and some are old. Some are single; some are married. Some are widows, and some are widowers. Some are divorced; some are broken and bereaved. Some are parents working and living in a single-parent home. Some are less fortunate people just doing the best they can. This creates an ideal way to learn from others' experiences. You could possibly find someone who is a lot like you or someone with similar experiences.

All are welcomed by Jesus to be a part of the Lord's *universal* church, and all are welcome at the *local* church too! Everyone is different! God made us that way, and He knows what we are (Psalm 103:13-14).

Many churches are filled with people with different personalities, but because everyone is on the same path loving and serving the Lord, the opportunity is there to develop deep friendships.

Just as people are not alike, so also are local churches different. You may be thinking how Free Will Baptists are different from other denominations. While that is true, Free Will Baptist churches can be very different as well. While Free Will Baptist churches share the common ground of our doctrine, that same document describes the ability for each church to determine the latitude for what is not described in the Treatise.

WHY LISTEN TO THE LEADERS?

Read Hebrews 13:17. What does it say about church leadership?

_____

Your pastor is first called by God to his profession and has prepared to be the shepherd of the congregation by diligent study and prayer. Although various pastors you know or have heard may fundamentally believe the same thing, they may deliver the message or teaching with different styles. Take every opportunity to learn from them. Ask questions. There is a reason a pastor is pastoring; He has been called and diligently studies the Word of God to help the people God has entrusted to his watch care.

If God still calls men to preach His Word and gives passion to others to teach His Word, then does God not call us to passionately listen (Nehemiah 8:1-3; 1 John 4:4-6)? When you listen, you then have an obligation to respond to what you now know.

Read James 1:22-25. How should you respond to the Scriptures you read and hear in church? What is the benefit for you?

_____

_____

WHY SMALL GROUPS OR SUNDAY SCHOOL?

Small groups or Sunday School can be a place you connect with people. In addition to a Bible study, you will find some of your closest friendships. People often group according to their age, location, life stage, age of their kids, or even by gender. However the groups are formed, find one in which you can most regularly attend and grow. People who join a small group or Sunday School class grow closer to God more quickly and to others in the church, causing a strong bond for you and your family.

In addition to connecting with people who will be a real source of encouragement and help, you will find the study in these groups helpful with everyday life. The Scriptures are filled with lessons to help you on your spiritual journey.

You may even find that your spiritual gifts allow you to become a teacher. Talk with your pastor about possibilities when you feel you are ready (2 Peter 3:18). If so, you will find blessings as you prepare lessons from the Bible and curriculum each week and the fulfillment of seeing the Holy Spirit apply the principles to the students you teach.

HOW DOES CHURCH HELP THE FAMILY?

Throughout the Old and New Testaments of the Bible, you will find multiple generations of the same families following and serving God. The combination of what you learn from church and your regular reading and study of Scripture at home will keep your family heading in the right direction. If we depend on what we get at our Bible classes, small groups, Sunday School, and church, we will not be depending on what God wants to give us on a daily basis. Involve your kids and teach them to love the Word of God through your example. Teach them to love church by your involvement and by your words of support.

What is the role of the pastor in your church?

_____

_____

Why should you be part of a small group study, small class, or Sunday School?

_____

_____

List ways you and your family will be involved in your local church starting now.

_____

_____

The pastor will help you grow in Christ. He ministers because he has a calling from God, and he desires to honor that calling. It is very important that you listen with a humble spirit and hungry heart so that you can grow in God's grace and in the knowledge of our Lord (1 Peter 5:1-3; 2 Peter 3:18). The pastor's relationship with the Word and with Christ should be so much a part of his life that it overflows into those around him. Likewise, that same love of the Word and of God should overflow into your kids and grandkids' lives. The greatest gift you can give is generational discipleship to your family tree.

You will encounter problems. These challenges will most likely come from relationships around you, attitudes you have, or another difficulty. Your pastor can be a resource and typically help you find answers through the Word of God. He can also offer counseling or refer you to counseling when needed. You should consult him spiritually in a similar way you consult your physician on physical matters.

BE THE CHURCH

Your trail ahead with Jesus can be treacherous. But as we have seen above, there's no need to travel it alone. Jesus has not rescued you to isolation, but community among all of His followers. With regular preaching and instruction from God's Word by His pastor servants, involvement in a small group or Sunday School class, and accountability with fellow Christ-followers in the setting of your local church, you are outfitted with all the necessary equipment to successfully arrive at your final destination. Go be the Church.

THE PERSON OF GOD

The ancient past was characterized by rampant polytheism, with various gods usually associated with particular areas of the world or particular causes (e.g., weather or fertility). People would experience good fortune one day and then devastation the next and conclude that a separate god was responsible for each outcome. In many an ancient mind, the world contained a multiplicity of gods.

Judaism and Christianity, however, are monotheistic, meaning only one God exists. The Jews to this day recite in their services the words of Deuteronomy 6:4 that state Israel must know there is but one God and one LORD. Paul stated there is one God (1 Timothy 2:5a). James revealed even the demons recognize only one God exists (James 2:19). When Moses penned the opening words of Scripture, he said in the beginning God created heaven and earth (Genesis 1:1). John expanded these words, explaining everything was made by Him (John 1:3a). Here we find no room for multiple deities, each contributing a part to the creative process. Rather, the Bible plainly presents the one God. All so-called others are fabrications of humanity's imagination. As *The Free Will Baptist Treatise of Faith and Practices* in Part II Chapter 2 states: "There is only one true and living God."

Because pagans believed in nonexistent deities, Scripture sometimes refers to "false gods" or "other gods," but it does so only to indicate the waywardness of people in so believing, not to endorse their existence. Thus, the first of the Ten Commandments instructs humanity to have no other gods but the one true God (Exodus 20:3). No others are permitted because no others exist. Paul explicitly stated in 1 Corinthians 8:4 that idols, which represented false gods, are in reality "nothing."

Alongside monotheism, the Bible also teaches an aspect of plurality regarding the nature of God. However a Christian understands this plurality, it must fit with the basic truth that there is only one God. We now focus on that plurality.

The Scriptures clearly assert that God exists in three persons: Father, Son, and Holy Spirit.

For example, we are instructed by Jesus to pray to the Father in heaven (Matthew 6:9). He told the woman at the well that people are to worship the Father in spirit and truth (John 4:23). Paul directed focus to the one God and Father of all (Ephesians 4:6). The Bible plainly asserts that God exists as a Father.

When people desire to be accepting or tolerant of many views, how can Christ- followers present to others that there is only one God—the God of the Bible?

_____

_____

Look at John 8:58, John 1:1. Did Jesus exist before being born in Bethlehem?

_____

Scripture also refers to the Son of God as being God. This is most easily seen in the attributes ascribed to Him. Jesus Himself said that He existed before Abraham (John 8:58). To open his Gospel, John referred to Jesus as the Word and stated that He existed "in the beginning" (John 1:1). So the Son existed in eternity past.

The Bible likewise presents the Son as having absolute control over nature. Winds obey his voice (Luke 8:25). Diseases flee at His touch (Mark 1:41). Even death gives up its prey at Jesus' command (John 11). He possesses all power. Jesus is also invested with complete rule over humanity. All the authority in heaven and earth is His (Matthew 28:18). None rank above Him. He also possesses all knowledge, even down to knowing people's thoughts (Luke 9:47). All truth is open before Him. Nothing is hidden.

These characteristics—eternality, power over nature, authority over humanity, knowledge of all things—are divine in nature and indicate that Jesus is divine. We are not left, however, having to piece it together that Jesus is God. Scripture states outright and repeatedly that He is. Thomas called Him his Lord and God (John 20:28). Paul referred to our great God and Savior, Jesus Christ (Titus 2:13). John stated that He is true God (1 John 5:20).

How do Jesus' attributes encourage you?

_____

_____

It will perhaps be helpful at this point to examine a few areas where confusion regarding the Son often springs up. The first relates to the Son's existing forever, and at no point did He come into existence. In the human realm, a son must necessarily come into existence after his father. This earthbound human rule, however, does not apply to God. The Son of the Father has existed throughout eternity. There was not a time when the Father existed alone and then somehow produced the Son. Rather, the Father and Son have always existed. Interestingly, the church father Athanasius (ca. 296–373) argued that unless the Son existed eternally alongside the Father, there was a time when the Father was not a father, and this could not be. Again, with created beings, fathers necessarily predate their offspring, but as Clement of Alexandria (ca. 150–215) said, the Son was "co-existent with the Father."[1]

Second, we should distinguish between the eternal existence of the Son of God and the coming into existence of the God-man Jesus. Only when the Son of God took on human flesh did the God-man, Jesus, come into existence. As noted above, the Son has existed throughout eternity, but His existence prior to the incarnation (taking on human flesh) was in spirit form.

Third, because Jesus is the *Son* of God does not mean He is inferior in nature to Father God. Some say, "The Son of God is not God but a son of God." However, note that Scripture presents Jesus as *begotten* of God (John 3:16). As C. S. Lewis aptly explained, to beget is to issue forth a like being. For example, birds *make* nests, but they *beget* birds. Man begets man. Therefore, what God begets is God. First-century Jews recognized this for they set about to kill Jesus because, as John puts it, He called God His Father, making Himself equal with God (John 5:18).

In one way, however, Jesus was subordinated to the Father: in His earthly role as Redeemer, He subjected Himself to the Father and took on a humble status, stating that the Father was greater than He (John 14:28). He was not alluding to His essential nature but to His role while on earth. Augustine (354–430) clarified this point: "Wherefore Christ Jesus, the Son of God, is both God and man; God before all worlds; man in our world . . . . Wherefore, so far as He is God, He and the Father are one [John 10:30]; so far as He is man, the Father is greater than He . . . As Word, He is equal with the Father; as man, less than the Father . . . . God without beginning; man with a beginning, our Lord Jesus Christ."[2]

So Christian faith maintains that both the Father and the Son are God, fully divine. The Bible also presents the Holy Spirit as God. The evidence here is not as clear as that regarding the Father and Son, but it is clear enough. Peter charged Ananias with lying to the Holy Spirit and, expanding on this statement, said this was lying to God (Acts 5:3-4). God's Spirit is said to be one who ascertains all truth (John 16:13). Paul uses the terms "God's temple" and "the temple of the Holy Spirit" interchangeably (cf. 1 Corinthians 3:16–17 with 6:19–20). Hebrews 9:14 refers to "the eternal Spirit," indicating the Spirit's existence back into eternity past. This same adjective is used of God in Romans 16:26. Finally, when delivering the Great Commission, Jesus commanded believers be baptized in the name of the Father, Son, and Holy Spirit, presenting the three as equals. So alongside the Father and the Son, the Holy Spirit possesses the attributes of deity.

How would you explain the relationship of Jesus the Son and the Holy Spirit to God the Father?

_____

_____

How does the fact that the Holy Spirit is deity practically impact a Christian's life?

_____

_____

We should pause to consider one heretical teaching of the Jehovah's Witnesses. They state the Holy Spirit is a force or power, not possessing personality. The Bible, however, is not on their side. We cited above the passage in Acts 5 where Ananias lied to the Spirit. Now ask yourself this question: Can a being without personhood be lied to? Interestingly, the Jehovah's Witness Bible, the *New World Translation*, muddies the water, charging Ananias with trying to "play false to the holy spirit." The verb they render "play false" in verses 3–4 is the Greek *pseudomai* and means to lie. In fact, the verb occurs in 10 other places in the New Testament. In the Jehovah's Witnesses' own translation, that verb is rendered in each of those 10 passages by some form of the English "lie." Only in Acts 5 do they employ an alternate verb.

We are left with the following scriptural assertions:

There is only one God.

The Father is God.

The Son is God.

The Holy Spirit is God.

From examining these statements, some charge Christianity with teaching things incompatible with one another. On the one hand, they say, Scripture presents only one God. On the other hand, three Gods. Which is it?

Some attempt to solve this apparent contradiction by understanding God to assume different roles at different times. This is called modalism, where sometimes God is Father, sometimes Son, sometimes Holy Spirit. He is like water (liquid, vapor, solid), they say, appearing in different forms. Scripture does not support this understanding. Father, Son, and Holy Spirit, according to the Bible, are distinct from each other and not merely different manifestations of the deity. The baptism of Jesus makes this clear. In the gospel accounts (Matthew 3; Mark 1; Luke 3), the Son is baptized, while the Father speaks approving words of His Son from heaven, and the Holy Spirit descends from heaven in the form of a dove and rests on Jesus. All three persons are present and distinct from each other.

Another erroneous analogy for God is the egg with its shell, white, and yolk, each a legitimate part of the egg. This approach, however, makes the Father, Son, and Holy Spirit "part" of God but not fully God. In the end, no proper analogy exists by which to understand God. Gregory Nazianzen (329–389) wrote long ago: "I have been unable to discover any thing on earth with which to compare the nature of the Godhead."[3] Our *Treatise* (Part II chapter 2) reflects this ancient truth when it states: "The mode of His [i.e., God's] existence . . . is a subject far above the understanding of man . . . . There is nothing in the universe that can justly represent Him."

The traditional way to handle the biblical statements on this subject is to recognize a plurality in a unity. God is one, but He exists as three persons—three that are characterized by perfect unity. Such a conclusion is not forced upon Scripture but actually springs from the biblical text. Note the plurality in the statement by God "let *us* make man in *our* image" (Genesis 1:26; see also Isaiah 6:8). Yet, as we have seen, the Bible says God is one. Jesus referred to His being "one" with the Father (John 10:30).

Scripture speaks of this plurality and unity of God in much the same way it does of the plurality and unity of husband and wife, who become one (Genesis 2:24). Dating back to the early church father Tertullian (ca. 160–ca. 220), this unity/plurality has been called the Trinity (tri-unity). Note that the term is not found in Scripture, as the Jehovah's Witnesses are quick to point out, but the concept it describes is. It is not the **term** *Trinity* that Christians insist on (though it is a fine term); it is the **truth** that term represents.

THE ATTRIBUTES OF GOD

We now turn to examine some of the attributes of God in an attempt to know what He is like. Ultimately He exists in such a multifaceted way that He can never be adequately described. At the same time, He has revealed Himself so we can grasp something of His glorious nature. He wants to be known and involved in your life and for you to be involved in His purpose.

The Bible teaches that God is wise. Paul exulted in the depth of the wisdom and knowledge of God (Romans 11:33). By this wisdom He laid the earth's foundations (Proverbs 3:19) and by this wisdom He unfolded the plan of redemption (1 Corinthians 2:6). What wisdom is involved in God's causing all things, even the self-willed acts of His creatures, to work together for good (Romans 8:28)! The complexity in this enterprise boggles the mind. Therefore, Scripture states that as the heavens are far above the earth, so God's thoughts are higher than humanity's (Isaiah 55:9).

The wisdom of God is such that He knows all things. This infinite knowledge, called omniscience, extends to all realms, leading to the title "God of knowledge" (1 Samuel 2:3). He sees where human eyes cannot penetrate (Joshua 7:1–11). He peers into the secret thoughts of people (Psalm 44:21). He knows the future before it comes to pass (Matthew 20:19). Hebrews 4:13 states that nothing is hidden from God, but all is laid bare before Him.

This is the longstanding testimony of the church. Clement of Alexandria wrote: "The Divine power, with the speed of light, sees through the whole soul."[4] The Reformer Theodore Beza said for one to try to comprehend the wisdom of God would only end in being "vehemently troubled and frustrated" since such an attempt was like trying to contain the ocean in a drinking cup.[5] The consistency of the Church's testimony merely reflects Scripture's clarity on this point.

In recent years, however, some in the Christian community have denied the omniscience of God. They say that if God knows all things, even what we will do before we do it, then we are not free to make real and meaningful choices. Without addressing all the intricate philosophical reasoning involved in such matters, let us simply note that to know something in advance is not to cause it to happen. As a father, sometimes I could see trouble brewing between my two sons in the room next door before the eruption of conflict. I surely did not cause their argument, but I could see it coming. In a similar yet absolute way, God knows in advance exactly what His creatures will do, yet He does not cause them to do this or that.

It should be noted that the Bible sometimes refers to God's coming down to earth *to see* what humanity was doing (Genesis 11:5). This and other such passages should be understood metaphorically with the meaning being that God was ceasing His attitude of ignoring what people were doing. Similarly, the gospels sometimes allude to Jesus' not knowing this or that (Mark 11:13; Matthew 24:36). One can understand this by examining the incarnation of Jesus carefully. Scripture presents Jesus as having two natures. He existed (and exists) as one person, but in Him resided both the human and the divine. He was not a hybrid, part God and part man. He was fully God and fully man, both at the same time. During His life, various aspects of these natures take center stage. Sometimes we see Jesus exercising divine prerogatives and driving out demons or stilling storms. Sometimes we see Him all too human, wearied from a trip or hungry for food. Both natures exist alongside each other. Perhaps this provides the basis for understanding passages that indicate Jesus didn't know something, like the day of His return to earth (Mark 13:32). In these instances, His human nature is in view. Had He chosen to know, He could have known for He possessed omniscience. Let me illustrate. Imagine one having all knowledge available to him simply by doing a computer search, say on Google. But then imagine this one with all knowledge at his fingertips deciding not to access certain information. No one fully understands the person of Jesus, but this illustration may help to explain the passages in question.

Before moving on, we should pause to consider the practical import of God's omniscience. Since He knows all things, it means we cannot hide our sins from Him. It means His love for us is in the context of His knowing intimately our every thought, word, and deed. It means He knows all the inner workings of the world so that He can wisely deal with our circumstances. Nothing will stump Him. It means He is equipped to mete out justice taking into account all the complexities of motives, circumstances, etc. Only an omniscient God can accomplish perfect justice. The wisdom of God is a most comforting doctrine.

Does the fact that God knows everything about you, your thoughts, your future actions and more, help you to stand in awe of His love for you?

_____

_____

How should your awareness of God's omniscience impact your daily actions, words, worries, concerns, relationships, fears, and joys?

_____

_____

Scripture also teaches that God is powerful. He can do all things, an attribute we call omnipotence. Jehoshaphat said power and might rest in God's hands (2 Chronicles 20:6). The mighty waves of the sea roll only as far as He ordains (Job 38:11). Nothing is beyond His reach and control (Jeremiah 32:17).

The power of God appears at its apex in His creative acts. The Bible teaches that out of nothing God made the worlds (Psalm 33:6, 9). He spoke creation into existence. In this astounding power, of course, God has no rival. We sometimes refer to people as being creative, but we really only mean they have the ability to think up interesting combinations of existing things. If you doubt this, try being creative and think of a sixth sense to add to our five. We can't even imagine another sense, much less create one. God, on the other hand, thought up all that exists. The great scientist Johann Kepler liked to say he was thinking God's thoughts after Him. The scientist only discovers what God first thought. But God not only contemplated the amazing system we call the universe. He created it! This truly is power.

Think of what God's omnipotence means in a practical way. It means that nothing is too hard for the Lord. When the children of Israel were hemmed in and could not escape the Egyptians, the Red Sea posed no problem for God. So our dilemmas fail to challenge the power of God. Is anything too hard for Him? No!

Omnipresence is another attribute of God. God is everywhere at all times. David said it did not matter where he went, God was there (Psalm 139:7–8). The Lord is not confined to a particular place at a particular time. Part of Him is not in one place and another part of Him somewhere else. He is always completely present everywhere (Deuteronomy 4:39). While your minds cannot grasp such an infinite presence, it at least helps to remember this is not a claim about a physical being but a spiritual one. Jesus' body, for example, is not omnipresent, but His spirit is.

The implications of this truth are wonderfully encouraging. The omnipresence of God means He is always with us. Joseph was locked away in an Egyptian prison, forgotten and abandoned by humankind. But the Lord was with him (Genesis 39:21). Jesus told His disciples He would be with them always (Matthew 28:20). We are never out of God's reach. Isaac Watts wrote:

> Within thy circling power I stand;
> On every side I find thy hand;
> Awake, asleep, at home, abroad,
> I am surrounded still with God.[6]

The Bible also describes God as holy (Leviticus 11:44; Revelation 3:7). At its root, this means He is in a category all by Himself, separate from all others (Exodus 15:13). There is no other like Him. This is true in every respect of His being. Not one is powerful as He is. Not one is wise as He is. Scripture especially indicates that God is distinct from all others in His moral perfections (Isaiah 5:16). He is holy in that He is just and righteous, unable to tolerate evil (Habakkuk 1:13). Where we are mired in sin, He is absolute purity.

Contemplating God's holiness leads us to rejoice in Him. We can imagine a being with absolute power and knowledge that is not righteous and good. We would quake before such an evil one. In God, however, the natural attributes of omnipotence and omniscience are joined with the moral attributes of purity and virtue. This leads us to worship. When we think of God's holiness, we recognize His holy nature sets Him apart from us; yet He joins Himself to us through the work of Jesus and the Holy Spirit. We are likewise comforted in God's opposition to all evil and injustice. Thomas Manton wrote: "You may sooner reconcile fire and water than God and sin." While for a time He allows sin free reign, one day He will make all things right.

How can a perfectly holy God have a relationship with a sinful person?

_____

_____

Another moral attribute of God is His love. Scripture employs many terms to describe this aspect of God's nature. He is gracious (Exodus 34:6), merciful (Psalm 78:38), kind (Jonah 4:2), and compassionate (Joel 2:13). Love ultimately is commitment to what is right and good for the one who is loved. It invests itself in the well being of others. The Bible thus teaches that God is committed to what is best for us. He loves us.

You should not think, however, that God's love for you means that your life will always be cushy and comfortable. As loving parents discipline their children, so the Lord disciplines you (Hebrews 12:6). First John 2:16 speaks of life as impacted by a sinful world. God will not remove the sin, but He will help you overcome it. You will never grow strong without facing adversity, so God, out of love, allows trouble to line your paths (Psalm 27:5). Though you may not sense it when you are in the fires of affliction, God is always superintending your lives with an absolute love.

The Bible also says God never changes. He is immutable (1 Samuel 15:29). He was not one kind of ruler in Old Testament days and another in our day. What characterized Him then, characterizes Him now (Malachi 3:6; Hebrews 13:8). The differences in approach God takes in dealing with His creation are prompted by His infinite wisdom, not changes in His character. In his poem "Andrew Rykman's Prayer," John Greenleaf Whittier wrote:

All things flow and fluctuate,

Now contract and now dilate.
In the welter of this sea,
Nothing stable is but Thee;
In this whirl of swooning trance,
Thou alone art permanence.[7]

God's immutability means that we can count on His always being wise and holy and good. If He changed with time, one day we could find yourselves before an unholy God or one without the power to affect His desires. Immutability joined with perfection is a blessed combination.

In conclusion, we should note that the various attributes of God are not in competition with one another. God's holiness should not be set against His love. In fact, while we single out this or that aspect of the nature of God, He actually exists as a perfect essence, not capable of division. He is not a compounded or composite being. He is what theologians call "simple." What we call the attributes of God are really just different ways of speaking of the great God who exists in perfect harmony with Himself and is incapable of being divided into parts.[8]

End Notes

[1]Clement of Alexandria, *Ante-Nicene Fathers*, 2.574.

[2]Augustine, *Nicene and Post-Nicene Fathers*, 1st series, 3.249.

[3]Gregory Nazianzen, *Nicene and Post-Nicene Fathers*, 2d series, 7.328.

[4]Clement of Alexandria, *Ante-Nicene Fathers*, 2.533.

[5]Theodore Beza, *A Little Book of Christian Questions and Responses*, trans. Kirk M. Summers, Princeton Theological Monograph Series (Allison Park, PA: Pickwick, 1986), 78.

[6]Isaac Watts, in *The New Laudes Domini: A Selection of Spiritual Songs, Ancient and Modern*, by Charles S. Robinson (New York: Century Company, 1892), p. 106.

[7]John Greenleaf Whittier, *The Complete Poetical Works of John Greenleaf Whittier* (Boston: Houghton Mifflin, 1894), p. 440.

[8]See Hermann Bavinck, *Reformed Dogmatics*, ed. John Bolt, trans. John Vriend, 4 vols. (Grand Rapids: Baker Academic, 2004), 2.173–77.

chapter 6

Your Guide—God
part 2

One of the more hysterical moments early in our marriage occurred after trying to teach my intelligent but sport's illiterate wife about basketball. We enjoy telling this story because my wife is now a big sports fan. I thought I had taught her well, but this was obviously not the case. While driving back from a trip during the NCAA playoffs, my brother and I wanted to know how our teams were doing that evening. What ensued would have surely won a prize on any television show as my wife answered my questions over the phone. As she described a touchdown, quarterback, and a home run in a basketball game we laughed until we almost had to pull off the road. She eventually admitted she did not know who was who or what was going on in the game. This classically illustrates the value of application. To know terms, labels, and definitions and not make application can be humorous in many situations. However, it is not funny when you fail to identify and apply the reality and identity of God in your life. Tragically, to not apply what you are learning about who God is will lead to perpetual spiritual infancy, discouragement, and a lack of a real relationship with your Savior.

As you apply the lessons that follow about the person of God, remember that God has intentionally revealed Himself to you in the Scriptures. In the Bible you see who God is and how He works.

There are two areas in which Christ-followers must be careful when discussing God's activity. The first is to think God is not *active* and to think of Him instead as *passive*. God is active. Some, by not *seeing* God at work, mistake this observation for God not *being* at work. In reality, God is absolutely actively at work. The second error occurs when you place on God your own expectations for what you think He should be doing. A question that some ask out of genuine hurt or honest curiosity is: If God is so loving, why did He not stop this? Too often these questions are based upon what that person assumes about God, and not what the Bible declares about Him. You must start with the truth of God's Word, and not your own preconceived notion of how God is supposed to act.

In the previous chapter, you learned who God is. In this chapter, you will see how He is at work in your life and other people's lives. Specifically, what does the Bible say concerning God in relationship to His activities, functions, and roles in the Scriptures? To help apply your knowledge, you will explore the following five roles of the Trinity: Creator, Redeemer, Convictor, Sustainer, and Encourager.

GOD THE CREATOR

The best place to begin is at the beginning. Biblically, that is the book of Genesis. Depending on your background, you may be inclined to skip this section as you have been led to believe that it has to do with science or subjects like evolution and creation. People often misunderstand much of what the Bible says about how humanity came to exist and God's role in creation.

In the first verses of the Bible, God declares that He directly and immediately created all that exists. He spoke, and creation began. Everything came from God as He created everything in six literal, 24-hour days (Genesis 1—2). The answers to the philosophers' questions about how people came to be and why humans exist are all found in the answer "in the beginning God created." As the pinnacle of God's creation, you are the focus of His love and affection, and you possess intrinsic value and dignity because God created you in His own image.

One of the more amazing points you see in Genesis 1 is the first mention of the Trinity. In these verses, you see God speaking. John 1:1-3 tells us that this is Jesus Christ the Son. God the Father is superintending creation and it is His power on display creating the world and humanity (Genesis 1:26). It was the Spirit of God who "hovered" above the waters (Genesis 1:2). All three members of the Trinity, God the Father, God the Son, and God the Holy Spirit are mentioned at creation.

God as the Creator is mentioned throughout the Bible (Psalms 19:1-4; 33:6-9; 135:5-7; Proverbs 16:4; Isaiah 42:5; Colossians 1:16-17; Hebrews 11:3; 2 Peter 3:5; Revelation 4:11). Some may consider this concept controversial. You may have friends who argue about creation and evolution. Please understand that the creation/evolution debate is not so much about science (although there certainly is a scientific element). The very definition of *scientific* is *that which can be studied and repeated for proof*, and neither creation nor evolution can be repeated in a laboratory. Belief in either requires faith; however, not believing in God-orchestrated creation attacks the trustworthiness of God's Word. At its source is the presupposition that either the world exists via purely natural means without God, or that it exists via supernatural means with God as Creator. If God is not the creator of everything, then God's Word cannot be trusted.

There are at least two other areas in which God's creative power is displayed. The first area is one that you have experienced recently. The Bible calls this the new birth (John 3:3-8). God has given you new life through salvation. You are a new creation (2 Corinthians 5:17). The verbs in the original Greek have the idea of progression or *becoming* new. God has made you a new creation, and He is still working on you! God has given you a new nature. You are no longer a slave to sin (Romans 6:17-18). God is doing a great work in your life that He will continue until Jesus returns (Philippians 1:3-6).

The second creative area is mentioned in Isaiah 65:17 and 2 Peter 3:10-13. At the end of time (not reality), God will create a new heaven and new earth. God will one day judge this sin-cursed earth and create it again in perfection. He is preparing a place for Christ-followers in His Father's house (John 14:1-2).

Practically, God as the Creator of all things teaches you several principles. First of all, it realigns your worldview. You can answer the philosopher's questions of origin, value, and purpose. God created you in His image to bring Him glory (Genesis 1:26; Colossians 1:16-17; Acts 17:24-27). You did not originate from animals or primordial microorganisms. Humanity did not come into being by random chance; you are a masterpiece of God's loving creation.

Second, God as Creator gives every person's life value and dignity. Society judges people by their appearance, performance, or wealth. The media fawns over the most outrageous and sadly the most sinful Hollywood stars and athletes. Society's values are certainly out of step with the Scriptures. Everyone has value and dignity, not because of their value to society, but because of their value innately created and assigned by God.

Third, as the Creator, He is the sovereign owner of all things and ruler of everyone. His sovereignty—that is, His absolute, total control and rule—is intrinsically tied to the fact that He created us (Revelation 4:11). Skeptics will concede that if God is the Creator, then of necessity, He would hold claim to how you live. God owns you. He made you. This certainly impacts your worldview as you come to understand that you belong to God by right of creation. Christ-follower or still lost—it really does not make any difference. All people are His by right of creation.

Who created everything that exists? How was it created? Why is God being the Creator so controversial? What is the real issue?

_____

_____

_____

Is the world more random and chaotic or ordered and designed? What does an orderly world reveal about God?

_____

_____

In what areas is God's creating power affecting you personally?

_____

_____

How does God as Creator give all human life dignity? How should this affect my view of others?

_____

_____

How does this speak to areas such as euthanasia, genocide, or abortion?
(For more about Evolution and Creation, Creation Science, and other helps see www. answersingenesis.org and www.icr.org).

_____

_____

_____

How do you explain to a friend who God is and what He does?

_____

_____

_____

GOD THE REDEEMER

For everyone who loves a good story, it is hard to top the story of redemption in the Scriptures. In this section, you will learn about God the Redeemer. *Redeemer* may seem like an unusual word because it is not used much today. Originally, it described a person who would buy back or redeem someone who was a slave. To be *redeemed* is to be bought from another for a set price. Typically this referred to those who were once enslaved. So, what does it mean when the Bible says that Jesus is your *Redeemer*?

Galatians 4:4-5 gives a wonderful overview of Jesus as Redeemer. At exactly the right time, God sent His Son Jesus to purchase or redeem you from your bondage. You were a lawbreaker, and as such, owed an overwhelming debt to the justice of God. If someone sins or does something wrong, there are only two options. One involves that person receiving just punishment for the crime committed; the other involves Jesus receiving the punishment in that person's place. Because God is both perfectly just and perfectly holy, forgiveness is only available through the cross of Jesus. When you were saved, your rescue was made possible because Jesus bore your punishment upon Himself on the cross. He redeemed you from the penalty of your own sins with His blood (Matthew 20:28; Acts 20:28; 1 Corinthians 1:30; Galatians 3:13; Hebrews 9:12; 1 Peter 1:18-19; Revelation 5:9). First Peter 1:18 describes it as "the precious blood of Christ." All that Jesus endured for you on the cross, including His ultimate death, was the *redemption price* for your sins.

Not only did Jesus pay the penalty for your sins, but His sacrifice also purchased you the wonderful blessings of His grace. You have freedom from the power of sin (Romans 6:18, 22). Simply stated, before you were saved you could *not* please God, but because of Jesus' redemption, you *can* now begin pleasing Him. His redemption gives you confidence in the face of death (Psalm 49:15). The Redeemer purchased you as His very own, and empowers you with a desire to do good works instead of sinful acts (Titus 2:11-14; Galatians 1:3-5).

The redemption of Jesus on the cross accomplished so many wonderful things on your behalf. You are now **justified** or legally in good standing with God the Father because Jesus has given you His righteousness (Romans 3:24). He provided His righteousness to you and took your punishment on the cross.

You have **forgiveness** because of the grace of God and the sacrifice so vividly pictured in His shed blood (Ephesians 1:7-8a). You are now relationally right with God as well as justified or legally right with Him.

Galatians declares you are now **adopted** by God, your new Father. In modern thinking, adoption means accepting someone who does not have a family into your own. The word for *adoption* in biblical times contained the idea of *being treated as an adult with all the rights and privileges enjoyed by the other adult family members.* When Jesus saved you, you received all of His forgiveness, all of heaven, all of the Holy Spirit, all of His peace, and all of God's grace. You immediately possessed all the privileges of being a child of God at the moment you were saved.

In today's society, children usually eat first at family gatherings since they need extra help, and when they are finished, they can play together while the grown-ups enjoy one another's company. Not too many years ago, the children either waited or were served at a separate table out of the way. It was a memorable experience for many children when they were finally allowed to eat at the *grown-up* table. In God's redemptive plan, from the moment you were saved, you have been "eating at the grown-up table" of His blessings.

Lastly, you are saved for the purpose of being a part of **God's special people** (Titus 2:11-14). You are no longer an outcast, no longer a stranger to the household of faith; you are part of the wonderful family of God. He has a special plan for you, a special home prepared for you, and a special way that He desires for you to live.

Often, I have reflected upon my parent's words as they would drop me off at a friend's house for a Friday night sleepover. "Remember who you belong to son," my dad or mom would almost always say as they got back in the car. Back then, it gave me pause as to my actions. It was a deterrent to being too rambunctious. In a different sense, now you can remember that you belong to the Lord Jesus Christ. It certainly is a help to do what is right, but it is a wonderful blessing to know that I am a part of His family and He is my heavenly Father.

Can you explain the balance of God's holiness and His grace? (What is His part and what is yours?) Why do you struggle with the concepts of perfect holiness and absolute justice?

_____

_____

What happened to your sins when you were saved? (Gal 2:20) Who paid the penalty on your behalf?

_____

_____

How does belief affect behavior? How does your redemption transfer into your lifestyle?

_____

_____

Which of the four blessings of redemption means the most to you? Why?

_____

_____

Why should you not shy away from terms like the cross *or the* blood *of Jesus? Why do some people refuse to use them?*

_____

_____

GOD THE CONVICTOR

When you hear the word *conviction*, you may think about the feeling experienced when you do something wrong. You may also be reminded of the feeling that occurs when a pastor is preaching or teaching the Bible, and you feel like he is talking directly to you about an area of sin in your life. In reality, this is the work of God in confronting you with truth, sin, and discipline. Your emotional response is really just one way to respond to God's convicting work. There are several responses from which you can choose, and sadly, not all of them are positive.

God's holiness, His hatred of sin, and His conviction of sinners are perhaps some of the most misunderstood or deliberately misconstrued realities concerning Him. "God wants you to be happy," "God loves you just as you are," or "Jesus told us not to judge" are all so-called "truths" that some people utter about God, but directly contradict His revealed character and convicting work. Many believe that Jesus is "all about love." They say that God would never want you to "feel bad about yourself." However, this is not a biblical perspective on God.

A common theme of the Old Testament is personal holiness (Leviticus 20:7). God gave the Ten Commandments as an absolute standard. These commands created a problem since all of humanity breaks God's Law with relative ease and frequency. Discussion of the penalty for breaking God's Law continues throughout the Old Testament and crescendos in Romans 6:23 when explaining that the consequence of sin is death, or eternal separation from God. But God, knowing humanity could not obey the command to be holy, sent prophets, preachers, and teachers to proclaim the need to repent. God used these people to lovingly show humanity its error so that they might be saved.

Jesus then came to call sinners to be sorry for their sins, and to ask God to forgive them for their wrongdoing (Matthew 4:17; Mark 2:17). Jesus lovingly draws all people to God because He alone is the way, the truth, and the life (John 6:44; 14:6). He went to the cross, and died for the sins of the whole world. God's desire is that no one should perish, but that all should come to repentance (2 Peter 3:9). If there is no conviction of sin or no realization of missing a standard, then there can be no real repentance.

The action of a person who is truly repentant is to turn away from what he or she is repenting of and to help this repentance he or she should turn to a replacement of this behavior. You repent of sin and turn to a practice of holiness in Christ's example.

Before you began following Jesus, God convicted you through the work of the Holy Spirit, who is perpetually at work pointing out sinfulness and the need for righteousness, and convincing individuals of coming judgment (John 16:7-11). Every person responds to God's conviction by either repenting or rebelling. This can been seen most clearly in Romans 1. The first half of the chapter speaks about the Gospel. The second half deals with people's responses to the Gospel. In Romans 1, all humans ask if there is a God as a result of nature or creation, and the Holy Spirit convicts and points them to the one Holy God.

You can see this easily in the dismissal of God's laws (the most famous are the Ten Commandments in Exodus 20). Even if you only focus on the Ten Commandments, you find that you cannot keep any of these perfectly without God's help. The truth is, everyone is excellent at breaking God's Law. When you break it, you may feel terrible temporarily, but the feeling can be suppressed. You then try to ease your conscience, but even though you enjoyed the sin, the nagging feeling of guilt never truly goes away. This is the work of God, using the Law to show you your sinfulness. His Spirit is drawing all people to confess their sins and to accept His offer of salvation.

Before you were saved, you would sin and not feel bad about it, but now you cannot enjoy sinful activities. Sins that used to be committed easily are difficult now because you know that you have offended God. This is the work of the Holy Spirit as He convicts you, changes you, and points out the sin in your life.

The practical work of the Holy Spirit is His introduction of non-Christ followers to Jesus. He now reminds you as a Christ-follower of the truth, and convicts you of offenses against God and others. As the Holy Spirit communicates with you in your heart, you can either respond by desiring more knowledge or by rejecting Him. The Holy Spirit may work through a sermon, an accountability partner, or your own Bible reading. You then realize the need for change—not for salvation, but to grow closer in your fellowship to God.

Define conviction. What is its purpose? How is biblical conviction different from feeling guilty (2 Corinthians 7:8-10)?

_____

_____

Why did Jesus preach repentance? What is repentance? Why did He die?

_____

_____

How does your response to conviction show the condition of your heart?

_____

_____

To help avoid constant battle over conviction, what can you do? (Philippians 4:6-8)

_____

_____

How does the conviction of a lost person or non-Christ follower and a Christ-follower differ? How are they the same?

_____

_____

_____

Name some of the roles or functions of the Holy Spirit.

_____

_____

GOD THE SUSTAINER

As we have already discussed, God is the Creator of all things and as such He is the Sustainer of all things. The laws of physics, thermodynamics, etc. all work as they should because He is in control of them. Cosmically, He is the One who keeps everything running just as it should. It is probably no surprise to you that God is intricately involved in helping you as a believer to "run as you should." He created you, but unlike a human inventor's creation, God's design allows for healing when you are hurt. In other words, your God is not looking from afar but is involved in the life of every created being, even mentioning His attention to the birds (Matthew 10:29–31).

Jesus tells several stories in Luke 11 that illustrate how He provides for your needs and sustains you. These stories highlight the marvelous truth that God does what is right for you because He is perfectly good and He perfectly loves you. God sustains you through the avenue of prayer, and He provides for you because of who He is, not because of what you need. As you look at the Old Testament, you will see many people who experienced God's provision. The prophet Elijah was tired, desperate, hungry, and lonely. God sent ravens to feed him. King David was hunted for crimes He had not committed and God sustained him. The prophets Jeremiah and Ezekiel experienced God's sustaining hand when it seemed their ministries were failures. The psalmist relates that he has never seen the righteous forsaken. Whether it is a physical or a spiritual need, God desires to strengthen and sustain you in your times of need.

God also provides for you in the area of holy living. God has given you everything necessary for life and godliness (2 Peter 1:3). You may not realize or take advantage of the tools that are provided, but you have everything you need to live for Him. After Jesus' death and resurrection, He told His disciples that He would give them *another* Comforter. The word *another* is used several ways in the original Greek. Here, it means *another of the same kind.* When Jesus ascended, the Holy Spirit was sent to those early Christ-followers, and to all who have followed Jesus ever since. You may be thinking that you would feel better and maybe even do a better job of being a Christ-follower if you just had someone to help you. God has provided not just principles and promises, but the person of the Holy Spirit to be your Helper. One of the Holy Spirit's functions is that of the Comforter. His title can literally mean *the One who is called alongside.* When no one knows how you feel or how to help you, the Holy Spirit does. Romans 8:26 even states that He will pray for you when you don't know how or what to pray! When no one can say what you need to hear, the Holy Spirit can whisper hope to your heart. The Spirit will use the Word to work in your life in every circumstance. He is your personal sustainer—emotionally, physically, and spiritually.

You can accurately say that God is all-sufficient. He's all you need. Part of your growth as a Christ-follower will be to discover that not only is He all you need in every situation, but also that He is all you want.

Why should prayer be your first response in good times and bad?

_____

_____

What is God's response to you when you come to Him in prayer? (Ephesians 3:12-21, Matthew 6:5-8, and Matthew 7:7-12)

_____

_____

The Holy Spirit is described as the Comforter. Describe the ways He sustains you in this role.

_____

_____

GOD THE ENCOURAGER

God has never been late, lost, or confused about who you are, and what you need. He loves you and knows everything about you. God knows your frame–your very makeup (Psalm 103:14). Your frailties, your sinfulness, and your worst and best are all known by God. Some people spend a great deal of time, money, and energy fixing up, hiding, or trying to keep hidden who they really are. Perhaps it is thought that if friends or colleagues discover the true *you*, they will not like what they see. God loved you when you were unlovely, lost in sin, an enemy of His, and deserving of death and Hell. Because He made you, He understands you. John 17 records Jesus' prayer for all future Christ-followers. It is an amazing thought to understand that before you were saved Jesus knew you, and prayed for you. One day you will be physically with Him when He returns (1 Thessalonians 4:16) and each day should be lived in anticipation of this.

On days that seem to not be wonderful, God promises He is working out all things for your good and for His glory. You may be tempted to wonder where God is when you are hurting. It is these times when you need to run to Him as fast as you can. His precious Spirit will comfort you and encourage your heart as only He can. Joy, one of the good gifts He gives, is different than happiness or even fun (John 15:11). You can buy *fun* at any amusement park in the country. *Happiness* can come or go depending upon your mood or your circumstances. However, *joy* does not depend upon your changing circumstances, but upon the unchanging character of God. To say this another way, your level of encouragement from God is not related to your personal situation, but your personal relationship. Paul and Silas sang in prison (Acts 16:25). Christ-followers through the centuries have praised God as they were martyred for their faith. You can have joy that abounds because you know Jesus. Your measure of encouragement is often proportionate to your fixation and meditation on God's Word, particularly His promises to you.

God constantly encourages you by His Spirit through His Word. In reality, you don't need different circumstances; you need the Bible to help you be different in your circumstances.

What are some ways that God encourages you?

_____

_____

How is grace not just a gift, but a necessity?

_____

_____

How are joy, happiness, and fun different?

_____

_____

How does the presence of God affect your circumstances?

_____

_____

John 17 and other passages talk about God helping you. How are each of these passages an encouragement? What promises are given that will help you today? (see verses 9–11, and 14–22)

_____

_____

_____

chapter 7

Your Destination

Robert Morgan & Dale Burden

By the power of Jesus' resurrection, and His payment for your sins, you have escaped the maze of sin. You are now on the path to His Kingdom. Here, in this final chapter, you will first gain a glimpse of your final destination: an eternal home with God called *heaven*, and then you will conclude by learning about several key points along your journey at which God has placed opportunities both for pausing to reflect on your progress as well as remembering how you came to be on this journey in the first place.

If you visit San Diego, you may notice a manicurist's shop called Heavenly Nails. Other parts of the country possess hotels that advertise their "heavenly beds." A popular restaurant in West Palm Beach is called Hamburger Heaven. There appear to be about 200,000 small businesses in the United States with the word *heaven* in their title, such as Heaven's Spa, Stationery Heaven, and, of course, Heavenly Hams. There is a coffee shop known as Heavenly Grounds, a business known as Heaven's Best Carpet Cleaning, a beautician with a shop called Heavenly Hair, and a dealer who calls his business Heavenly Hot Tubs. Obviously, our culture ascribes great value to any product or experience, which associates itself with the concept of heaven, but what and where is heaven according to the Bible?

THE NEW HEAVENS & NEW EARTH

A good place to start your study of heaven is Revelation 21-22. In these two chapters, the apostle John is describing the conclusion of time, the beginning of eternity, and the experience of heaven, which he was privileged to witness as Jesus revealed it to him through a vision. John saw that the current heavens and earth are passing away. There is coming a day when the entire starry sky—the celestial universe and the outermost reaches of space—will collapse (Isaiah 34:4; 2 Peter 3:10-13; Revelation 6:12-17). The current heavens and earth are temporary, transient, winding down, slowing up, and burning out. At the dawn of eternity God is going to re-create the universe. There will be a new expanse of heaven; new stars and planets and comets and constellations; new galaxies and quasars and burning tapers in the sky. While it may boggle your mind to think of what the new heavens are going to be like, it is clear that God is going to recreate the universe and equip it for eternity.

When other religions or philosophies speak of our eternal destination they use abstract and nebulous terms, like the hereafter, utopia, nirvana, destiny, the otherworld, the great unknown, lotus land, and the happy hunting ground; but the Bible uses a very earthy word—earth. *The new earth will be a place of beauty.* If this old sin-cursed, polluted, spoiled, aging world is so beautiful now, can you imagine the pristine beauty that will surround us throughout eternity when God re-creates the world without sin, death, decay, or the curse? There will be beauty without measure on the new earth. *The new earth will be a familiar place.* Scripture supports the idea that the new earth will have some of the same features as the old. Here are some of its features:

1. Mountains: *Revelation 21:10 indicates that the Spirit carried John to a mountain great and high, and there showed him the Holy City, Jerusalem, coming down out of heaven from God.*

2. Rivers: *One such river is described in Revelation 22:1. It is a crystal river whose headwaters flow from the very throne of God.*

3. Tree-lined City Streets and Boulevards: *Revelation 22:2 indicates the city Heaven will have such streets. It seems likely that the vast new earth, likely larger than our present one, will have other cities. These cities will be peaceful and unpolluted places free from crime, hatred, and violence.*

4. Jewels and Precious Stones: *These are described for us in Revelation 21.*

5. Animals: *If God took so much delight in creating the animals when He made the earth in the beginning, why would you expect Him to forget about them on the new earth? Some aspects of the millennial earth seem to preview the new earth. One of these is the peaceful coexistence of animals and people as described in Isaiah 11:6-9.*

6. No Sea: *Some theologians and scientists believe that the oceans as we know them today were not part of God's original design for planet earth, but were formed by the great flood of Noah's day and represent judgment. The oceans take up three-fourths of space on this* *planet, and the entire human race is restricted to the final one fourth. However on the new earth, the total planet will be beautiful, verdant, and capable of habitation. Surely in the new created order God will provide a place for His dazzling and colorful sea creatures. Likely, you will be able to snorkel and dive and immerse yourself in the waters of the new earth, but these enormous expanses of vast, cold, dark ocean waters will be gone. The new earth is going to be much more habitable than that.*

When you think of heaven, don't think of some nebulous, cloudy place where you'll be participating in nonstop church services. Think of a literal, physical universe, a new planet earth with mountains and rivers and cities and animals. Heaven is going to be earth—the new heaven and new earth. It is going to be tangible, touchable, beautiful, and eternal. It is for you and all other Christ-followers to experience and enjoy because you know Jesus Christ as Lord and Savior.

Of all the verses you have just read about Heaven, which one is your favorite and why?

_____

_____

Thinking about spending eternity with Christ in the beauty of Heaven with everyone, how would you describe Heaven to a child?

_____

_____

THE NEW CITY

In addition to the new heavens and new earth, John writes about heaven being the new city—New Jerusalem. When you read through Revelation 21 and 22, you find that the word *city* occurs 12 times. A city is a literal place with people and streets and trees and buildings and parks and cultural venues and so forth, all subject to a common government. It is a concentration of people living in one geographical area with all the infrastructures that makes that possible. If the word *city* in this chapter means anything, it means that. This literal city exists in the here and now. It is where believers go when they die; and in eternity this city will descend to the New Earth becoming its capital city.

The new heavens are in the future. The new earth is in the future. You have likely attended a wedding and watched as the groom entered, then the bridal party entered, and then there was a meaningful pause. The music changed as the great moment arrived. The bride's mother stood, everyone else stood, and the bride regally marched down the aisle to be united with her groom. This is the picture the Lord uses to help us visualize this great, shimmering, white, bright city descending down the aisle of blinding beams of light and being united with the eternal earth. As the bride glides down the columns of light to the new earth, a herald announces the great message of God will dwell with His followers (Revelation 21:3).

Right now there are two realities—heaven and earth. There is the spiritual world and there is the physical world. When the times reach their fulfillment (Ephesians 1:10), God will merge the two realms together. The highest heaven will be vacated, as it were, and the Lord will relocate. Heaven and earth will become one. God will dwell with you and the great host of others who have commenced the journey you are on with Jesus. You all will live with Him forever.

THE NEW ORDER

The final "new" thing in Revelation 21:1-4 is the new order. Sometimes this life is so painful, you struggle to go on; you would almost rather die than face some of the burdens and the sorrows and the pressures that come your way. In heaven, none of those things will ever trouble you. No more death. No more sorrow. No more pain. No more crying. The old order of things will be passed away, and a new order will be established. All the stress, strain, crying, and pain will be over—and there will be no more death.

The events and descriptions in the book of Revelation are so fantastic and fabulous that the writer is continually stopping to reassure you that these things are actually true. This explains the repetition of two words that show up all throughout this book, "faithful," and "true." Can you take the descriptions of the heavenly city literally? The answer is a resounding, "yes!" Is the fountain of the water of life described in these verses literal or figurative? It may be both. A literal description would fit nicely with the existence of the crystal river flowing from Throne Square in the center of the city. Is the fountain figurative? It certainly has a figurative meaning as well. It is the fountain filled with the water of life given to all who thirst.

Will you eat and drink in heaven? It would certainly seem so. God created human beings in Genesis 1 with the capacity of eating and drinking. God created the joy of eating and drinking. The pattern and model for your resurrection and eternal body is the post-resurrection, glorified body of Jesus. As you study the glorified body of Christ, you can learn a lot about the way your own body will function on the new earth. Luke 24:36-43 indicates that in His post-resurrection body Jesus ate. Our Lord demonstrated to His disciples that His resurrection body was identifiable, physical, literal, recognizable, and fully capable of enjoying food and drink. You may take the description of the river in Revelation, which is called the River of the Water of Life, literally as well. It may very well be the primary water source of the New Jerusalem.

There will be no sin in heaven. Revelation 21:8 serves as a warning. As a warning, it explains that unless individuals receive the forgiveness of sin purchased for them on Calvary's cross, they cannot enter heaven. Without Jesus, you belonged on this list as well. Who has not on occasion been a coward? Who has not harbored doubt and unbelief? Who has not been abominable, murderous, or immoral, at least in their hearts? Who has not committed idolatry by loving some other object more than Christ? Who has not lied? Everyone, including you, has, and those sins marred your soul and disqualified you from heaven. However, on the cross Jesus took your sin upon Himself. That is the genius and the beauty of the atonement. Your only hope was to receive Jesus as Savior. The Bible says there is no other person who has ever inhabited this planet (or ever will) through whom you can obtain this rescue (Acts 4:12).

Revelation 21:8 also offers a blessing. It means that there will never be a single murder committed in heaven, and there will be no fear of one ever occurring. There will be no unbelief, no lying, and no idolatry. It will be a world without sin.

You will not be able to sin in heaven. Sin always results in death and separation from God. There will be no death in heaven because there is no sin there. You will not only be unable to sin, you will not want to sin or even want to want to sin. Will this violate your free will? No. The inability to be something does not inherently violate your free will. You might wish you lived in the 16th century. You might wish you had been born someone else. You might wish you had wings. Those are impossibilities. That they are impossibilities does not violate your free will. God cannot sin, yet He possesses a sovereign will. There will be no temptation in heaven. There will be no evil in heaven. You will have no evil desires within you. There will be no Satan in heaven. There will be no demons in heaven. There will be no sin or sinners in heaven. You will have the righteousness of Jesus who died and rose again once for all to do away with sin.

Ultimately all your sorrows and heartaches come from sin—either your own sin or the sin of another. None of that will be there, not a scrap of it, not ever. All the effects of sin will be gone, and this old sin nature, the one that constantly troubles and pulls us down, will be banished forever.

ANTICIPATING ETERNAL GLORY

The apostle Paul writes of an experience, possibly a vision, in which heaven was witnessed firsthand (2 Corinthians 12:1-5). It is unclear whether Paul is describing a view of heaven from his own experience or if he is recounting it from a friend's witness. However, it is clear that Paul possessed a vibrant understanding of his eternal home in heaven. He seemed to have no fear of dying. He expressed great anticipation for going to be with the Lord, and in light of heaven, the trials of this world were much less daunting; for His attention was fixed, not on the light and momentary afflictions, but on his exceeding and eternal weight of glory. Paul referenced this hope again and again in his letters to the churches. He explained that all Christ-followers, including you today, live in a fallen world where decay and death are inevitable realities. However, in the life to come you will have a new, eternal, incorruptible, resurrected body (Romans 8:23-25). Furthermore, he wrote that when you face the death of one who knows Jesus you do not have the hopeless grief of never again seeing the one you loved. Instead, you have the passing grief of one who anticipates a glad reunion to come (1 Thessalonians 4:13-14). Paul knew that once you have come to faith in Jesus Christ–confessing your sin and accepting His sacrifice on your behalf–you look forward with eager anticipation to spending eternity with Him. This hope of heaven infuses every Christ-follower with joy in this life (Colossians 1:5).

We are all by nature afraid of dying, but Christ-followers gradually replace their apprehension of dying with anticipation for this City Foursquare whose builder and maker is God, and anticipation is a wonderful thing. Keep your eyes on Jesus, your trail Guide, as you anticipate this glorious destination.

List some items that will not be in Heaven.

_____

_____

Having studied Heaven a little deeper, how does that help you face death with less concern as a Christ-follower?

_____

_____

OVERVIEW OF MEANINGS OF ORDINANCES

When hiking in the mountains, there are occasional overlooks at high elevations that afford you a glimpse to the valley below. The Creator placed overlooks there for a purpose. Pausing to ponder the purpose is inspiring and important.

There are similar places the Christian will encounter in your hike toward heaven. Places where you can look back at how far you have safely come and marvel at God's amazing grace. At such places you can gaze heavenward and see what still lies ahead.

The ordinances God has ordained for His people provide such occasions of an overlook. In the simplest sense, an ordinance is a celebratory observation or ceremony instituted by Jesus Christ, practiced by the early church, and clearly taught in God's Word. Ordinances are practices that represent something greater than the actual practices themselves. They are earthly symbols that reflect eternal truths. Three simple services, observed according the Lord's instructions, will speak volumes to you regarding your entire journey from earth to heaven, serving to remind you of your condition before becoming a Christ-follower. The first two display the infinite price paid to redeem or rescue you from your sins. The third will teach you humility, service, and a daily cleaning of one's self spiritually.

THE ORDINANCE OF BAPTISM

This first overlook comes at the very beginning of your hike: believer's water baptism. Baptism is a ceremony, which is performed by another follower of Christ—a pastor or other church leader—who fully immerses you and then raises you once again up from the water.

THE MEANING OF BAPTISM

The apostle Paul makes the tangible illustration of baptism so clear in Romans 6:3-4, where he describes baptism as the picture of being buried and resurrected like Jesus. Notice these verses describe baptism as co-identification with Jesus as well as a portrait of the radical transformation that took place when you became a Christian. The ordinance of baptism is an outward, physical picture of a previous inward, spiritual baptism by the Holy Spirit.

Be careful you do not confuse *spiritual* baptism with the physical baptism. The *spiritual* baptism by the Holy Spirit is better understood as an *invisible reality*. Although you look and perhaps even feel the same after becoming a Christ-follower, the invisible reality is that you died to sin's bondage and were spiritually resurrected with Jesus at that moment. Baptism places that spiritual reality into a physical symbol, which you and others can see and know.

This is similar to a wedding ring, which is a physical symbol of an invisible, spiritual union between a husband and wife. The Holy Spirit identifies us and places us in Christ before we are ever baptized in water. Both Titus 3:4-7 and 1 Corinthians 12:13 further explain this spiritual reality. This later passage makes it clear every believer receives this spiritual baptism at the time of salvation.

THE METHOD OF BAPTISM

The word *baptize* is an English transliteration of the Greek word *baptizo,* which was predominantly used by Greek writers to mean to immerse, to sink a ship, or to sink (in the mud), to drown, or to perish in water.1 When Jesus was baptized, Mark describes Him emerging from the water (Mark 1:9-10). When John the Baptist was baptizing, the Bible states he selected the location specifically because there was a significant amount of water there (John 3:23). This implies that enough water was needed to immerse the person being baptized. Thus, most historians agree the method of baptism in the early church was baptism by immersion.

THE MOTIVE FOR BAPTISM

It is clear throughout the New Testament that baptism is motivated by the desire to identify with Jesus (Romans 6:1-4). Baptism is a public statement that a person has by faith, received Christ as Savior, desires to identify with Him and publically testify of this commitment. All Christians should pursue baptism as a public commitment to their new association with Jesus.

A second motivation for pursuing baptism is that it is a command to all believers. In Matthew 28:18-20, the Lord commanded His followers to do three things: share the Good News of Jesus with others, baptize those who believe, and teach them to observe His commands. As you read the New Testament, you see baptism was the immediate response of believers of their love for Jesus.

Water baptism is not a *means* of salvation nor is it a *necessity* for salvation. It is simply, yet significantly, a *testimony* of salvation. Once you have been forgiven of your sins, you are not ashamed of Jesus. You want others to know about your new life in Christ. After salvation, baptism is the first act of obedience and fulfills that purpose.

Have you been baptized? (If not you might consider talking to your pastor about this event in your life)

_____

Who would you invite to your baptism service? (Family, friends, this could introduce Christ to your guests who are not Christ-followers)

_____

THE ORDINANCE OF COMMUNION

Communion or the Lord's Supper is the second ordinance. During the Jewish Passover, Jesus instituted this permanent, lasting observance for all people who trust in Him. The Passover meal had previously been established to celebrate and remember the Jewish deliverance from Egyptian bondage. The purpose of the Lord's Supper is to celebrate the greater deliverance of Christ-followers from their sins.

THE CAUSE FOR COMMUNION

Beginning in verse 23 of 1 Corinthians 11, the apostle Paul describes the meaning of this blessed service. Like baptism, the motivation for participating in the Lord's Supper is identification with and love for Jesus, and obedience to His instruction. The two elements—the broken bread and the cup containing the "fruit of the vine" (Matthew 26:29; Mark 14:25; Luke 22:18)—are symbols of Christ's broken body and shed blood, reminding us what our salvation cost.

When Jesus was crucified, His body was brutally wounded, disfigured, and broken. The crimson contents of the cup speak of His shed blood (Isaiah 53:5; John 19:34). However, the greatest pain Jesus endured was taking your sins upon Himself, which resulted in His holy, heavenly Father turning His back on Him. The reason Jesus took on flesh and blood was so that He might die for your sins. When you observe communion, you are reflecting on and remembering what Jesus did for you on the cross. Truly, the Lord's Supper should be a serious and sacred occasion.

THE CONTEMPLATION OF COMMUNION

The Lord's Supper provides a believer a time to contemplate what Jesus has done for him or her.

Look Within

Communion is a time for you to examine yourself (1 Corinthians 11:28). This is not an examination by the church. It is the Lord's Supper, not the church's. If you are the Lord's child and right with Him, you are welcome at His table. Caution is given that this must not be done irreverently or in an unworthy manner.

To prevent this, Paul reminded them of some of the serious consequences that had befallen them for abusing this sacred service (1 Corinthians 11:30).

Look Around

Communion is also a time to reflect on our relationship with one another as well.

In 1 Corinthians 10:16-17, Paul teaches that communion is meant to be a shared experience, showing our need for one another. Before taking part, ask yourself if there is any unforgiveness in your heart toward a fellow follower of Christ.

Look Ahead

Communion reminds us of the promised return of Christ. He said the next time He would take part in communion would be in His established kingdom (Matthew 26:29; Luke 22:18; Mark 14:25). Our participation reminds us of Jesus' promise. Communion will help make Jesus' death real for you until He returns (1 Corinthians 11:26). Before you take communion you should ask yourself if you are ready for the return of Jesus Christ.

The Bible does not state how often the Lord's Supper should be observed. It only tells us that we should observe it regularly. For some, that is weekly, some quarterly, and others annually. To every follower of Christ, the command is clear: Do this while remembering Christ (1 Corinthians 11:24–25). If you are avoiding His table, you need to ask: What do I need to get right?

Read Matthew 27 or John 19 (Both chapters are about the details of Christ's crucifixion) and note what details communion reminds you to never forget in this story.

_____

_____

Consider using a communion service to talk with your kids about Christ's gift of salvation through His death. (Make some notes here for what you might say)

_____

_____

THE ORDINANCE OF FEET WASHING

The third and final overlook in this journey is the ordinance of feet washing. Jesus introduced feet washing to His disciples (John 13) shortly following the Lord's Supper. Only hours before the cross, He used a basin of water and a towel to teach the disciples a vital lesson regarding what their future service would require for it to be effective. See Chapter XVIII of the Free Will Baptist Treatise.

THE PRACTICE OF FEET WASHING

After washing the disciples' feet, Jesus said you should follow His example and practice this on a regular basis (John 13:14-17).

The practice of washing a person's feet, often performed by servants during the cultural period of the Bible, depicts a relationship of humble service between you and others and the identification with your Master Jesus.

THE PRINCIPLES OF FEET WASHING

Humility is the first great principle we learn from this ordinance. The task of washing a guest's feet was considered a degrading job, to be performed only by the lowest of servants. Jesus' example of feet washing was intended to capture the humility of associating with the lowest status in order to serve others. This humility is most supremely recognized by the incarnation of Christ. Jesus' washing the disciples' feet depicts, in a real way, the humiliation of Christ when He "humbled" Himself, condescending to become a man and a servant to man (Philippians 2:5-11). Paul wrote, we are to share the mind of Christ (verse 5). His mind set no limit to what He would endure to help you find the start to this journey and walk with you each step of the way. By the genuine practice of this ordinance you can manifest the same spirit of humility that we find in our Savior and be reminded that He took on the form of a servant when He came to be one of us.

Feet washing also depicts sanctification by pointing to the need for continual cleansing in the life of the believer (John 13:10). You acquire "dirt" during your journey through this sinful world. John states that faithful confession of sin results in faithful forgiveness and cleansing on the basis of Jesus' shed blood (1 John 1:7, 9). Feet washing illustrates this. It is a constant reminder of your need to live clean and holy on your continued hike.

THE PROBLEMS WITH FEET WASHING

Many feel that the practice of feet washing was just a custom of the day and was never intended to become an ordinance of the church. It was indeed a custom of that day, but one performed by a servant, not the master. However, after Jesus specifically encouraged His disciples to continue His example, Scripture records the church continued the practice (1 Timothy 5:10). Many of the early church fathers also spoke of the church practicing feet washing (see *Free Will Baptist and the Washing of the Saints' Feet*, a pamphlet written by the Free Will Baptist Historical Commission as part of the Free Will Baptist Heritage Series: Foundations of Faith and Practice).

Although the lessons of humility, incarnation, and sanctification are more important than the act of feet washing itself, this is true of all of Christ's ordinances. Each ordinance points to a reality greater than the act itself. Feet washing is meaningless apart from the reality it represents.

Feet washing remind you of relationships with others around you. Can you say most of your interaction with others shows a humble attitude? Recall a time when a humble attitude was evident and how that impacted the relationship.

_____

_____

Feet washing reminds us of a daily cleansing spiritually not for salvation but forgiveness of sins we have committed. Have you built in a regular time of prayer that includes going humbly to God asking forgiveness each day?

_____

_____

CONCLUSION

Christ commanded all of the ordinances. He personally set the example, and the early church practiced these. Those who have learned what they teach and have faithfully practiced them have found His promise of happiness to be true (John 13:17).

Baptism pictures our salvation by faith in Jesus' finished work, resulting in your identifying with Him symbolically in His death, burial, and resurrection. The Lord's Supper makes what He did on the cross very real and will enhance your relation with Him by a regular self-examination. Washing of the saints' feet teaches the enjoyment of effective ministry to others, humility, and daily cleansing are all essential. Since the time of Christ, heavenward hikers have found that time spent at these divinely designed overlooks has strengthened their faith and increased their determination to finish their course with joy (Acts 20:24). You will find participating in each to be special when reflecting on the meaning of each ordinance and how each will help you on your journey.

End Notes

[1] *Theological Dictionary of the New Testament*, ed. Gerhard Kittel, Geoffrey W. Bromiley and Gerhard Friedrich, electronic ed. (Grand Rapids, MI: Eerdmans, 1964-).

Your Obstacles

Rising to a height of 1,350 feet, Mount Nebo stands outside a small town in the River Valley of western Arkansas. One hot July day during my time in the area serving as a pastor, my family and I decided to spend time at Mount Nebo State Park. We were looking to have a fun, adventurous day hiking one of the many trails surrounding the park. Since my kids were young, I asked the park ranger for an easy trail. He pointed me to the trailhead of a hike he thought we could complete in under an hour.

So off we went.

Midway through the hike there was a smaller path leading away from the main one that, according to the sign, led to a natural spring. I envisioned a small pool of water, a place where we could cool off, and maybe get a drink. The sign said it was just one-quarter of a mile. What the sign did not say was the path went straight down hill, which meant a steep climb on the return. Once we reached the spring, we were terribly disappointed. The spring was a shallow mud hole the size of dinner plate! By the time we climbed back up the hill to the original path, my children were in tears; the one-hour hike ended up being three hours long. My family has never gone hiking with me since!

SATAN
The Deceiver

The Bible says you have a fierce enemy named Satan whose sole intent is to bring you to destruction. How does a story about a failed hiking attempt relate to Satan?

Satan is a deceiver—it's one of his main characteristics. Like the sign promising a spring that led to a mud hole, so Satan promises one thing but delivers another. Satan deceived Adam and Eve into eating the forbidden fruit (Genesis 3:1-7). He tried to deceive Jesus into believing he had the power to give Jesus the world (Matthew 4:9). One day in the future he will deceive the entire planet (Revelations 12:9). Satan is a master deceiver.

Now that you know deception is Satan's main characteristic, how, and in what ways, do you think you have been a victim of his deception?

_____

_____

The Finite Enemy

Have you ever thought Satan was God's evil twin? According to the Bible, that is not true at all! First and foremost the Bible teaches that Satan was a created angel (Ezekiel 28:13).[1] Recognizing he is a creature, created by God, is important because it means he is not an eternal being. Satan is not the opposite of God. Satan does not share the same power and authority as God. Satan is not *omniscient* (all-knowing; he does not know everything, and he cannot read your thoughts), *omnipotent* (all-powerful; he cannot get you to do anything you do not want to do), or *omnipresent* (all-everywhere; Satan can only be at one place at one time). On the other hand, God is all of these at all times. As a created creature, Satan is not even close to being equal with God!

The Rebel

Although Satan was created by God, he was a special creation. Satan enjoyed an exalted position in the court of God, ordained by God as a high angel (Ezekiel 28:14-15). As a creation of God, he was perfect, but he was not content. Satan was full of pride. He did not want to serve God; he wanted to be God. Satan rebelled against God and was kicked out of heaven, along with the angels that sided with him in his attempted coup (Ezekiel 28:16-19; Isaiah 14:12-17). The Bible says one-third of the angels followed Satan (Revelation 12:4). Thus, while Satan can only be at one place at one time, through his comrades (the other fallen angels, called "demons") his presence is felt over all the earth.

While Satan is not God, nor the opposite of God, he is a powerful creation of God who presently roams the earth, influencing world systems, human ideology, governments, world religions, and man-made media. However, he is not to be feared, and he can be overcome.

When you placed your faith in Jesus Christ, the power of the Holy Spirit indwelt you, and the

Bible tells us that the presence of God within us is greater than the presence of evil around us (1 John 4:4). Presently, Satan's mission is to roam this planet creating havoc, thwarting the expansion of God's kingdom on earth, and detouring believers on their faith journey through this present life (1 Peter 5:8).

The Liar Tempter

How does Satan attempt to thwart God's plan and detour believers?

As we have already seen, his primary technique is deception, but he has a backpack full of tools for his trade. (Fortunately, the Bible tells us about those tools.) Satan pulled out all his gadgets when he tempted Jesus (Matthew 4:1-11).

Matthew used three words in his retelling of Jesus' temptation to describe Satan. The first word is *devil* (Matthew 4:1). The New Testament word translated *devil* is *diablos*, which means *slanderer* or *accuser* and refers to a person who brings untrue indictments against another person. He stands before God, as he did in the book of Job, bringing false accusations against God's servants (Job 1:3-11). He whispers in your ear, "You are nothing but a failure and a hypocrite. You don't deserve God's grace. You have made too many mistakes for God to use you. If people really knew what you were like, they would hate you. Who do you think you are? You are no better than anyone else."

How do you respond when you hear those whispers?

_____

_____

Satan slanders followers of Christ, accusing them of not being worthy of love, grace, and forgiveness. Satan tries to convince followers of Christ to believe they are still condemned and destined to hell instead of forgiven and on their way to heaven (Romans 8:1, 37-39).

The next word Matthew used is *tempter* (Matthew 4:3). The word *tempter* is a legal term, and fits well the context of what was taking place. In the wilderness, Satan put Jesus on trial. Acting as a prosecuting attorney, Satan tried to deceive Jesus by bringing false charges against Him, testing His resolve, getting Jesus to doubt what He knew to be true.[2]

Satan does the same thing today. Before you turned to Jesus, Satan tried to convince you that you were OK, your sins weren't really all that bad, and you were just being yourself, enjoying life. Before your faith in Jesus, Satan was your defense attorney. Now, as a follower of Jesus, Satan is a prosecuting attorney. Satan puts you on trial, and tries to convince you that you are guilty and lost in your sins. He tries to get you to doubt God's Word and to question what you know to be true.

In what ways have you experienced Satan's cross-examination in your life?

_____

_____

The next word is the name, *Satan* itself (Matthew 4:10). The name means *adversary*. Ultimately, as a follower of Jesus, Satan is your enemy. He is your antagonist, your attacker, and your opposition. He stands in your way, trying to keep you from hiking the path, or finishing the race, or climbing the mountain is in front of you. The equipment he uses to assault you includes deception, slander, and false accusations, and he uses these tools to attack you on three fronts.

His three fronts are summarized in 1 John 2:16 and can be categorized as passions (or lusts), possessions, and pride. Satan knows the best time to attack your passions is when you are tired. It is when you are exhausted and your defenses are down that your lusts can lure you down a dangerous path. When an appealing temptation comes your way, and you think, "if it feels good, do it," your passions are being assaulted.

Share a time in your life when strong temptations followed physical exhaustion?

_____

_____

_____

What are the areas of your life where you are most vulnerable to temptations?

_____

_____

What can you do now that will help you avoid giving in to your lusts and passions?

_____

_____

If Satan can't detour you off the trail by appealing to your desires, he will try to detour you by giving you all the things you think you need. Sometimes, the material items we value as blessings from God are really a curse from the enemy. Remember, Satan is an excellent deceiver, and often his deception says, "Go ahead, this will make you look good." When you hear that temptation, you are being attacked by the power of possessions.

Is there an item you find yourself thinking about having to the point it takes up a great deal of think time? (Overly strong desire to have something)

_____

_____

How do you combat the temptation of materialism in your own life?

_____

_____

Satan tries to trip you up by convincing you that you are superior to others because of your religious practices. Satan will try to convince you that God needs you, and that your church would fall apart without you. He sets you up and then knocks you down with your own hypocrisy.

Every time Satan attacked, Jesus fought off the attack by quoting God's Word (Matthew 4:4, 7, 10). The primary weapon you possess for defeating the one who wants to destroy you is the Bible. The best way to overcome temptations is to study, read, memorize, and apply Scripture to your life. The closer you are to God, the better you are able to handle life's twists and turns. In the same way studying a map will keep you on course while backpacking, so studying the Bible will keep you on course in your spiritual life.

Jesus died for you, God has forgiven you, and the Holy Spirit lives inside you. With all the power of the Godhead residing within you and God's Word lighting your path (Psalm 119:105), you can overcome every trial and temptation Satan throws your way. Satan may rule the world, but he no longer has dominion over you. You can overcome him when he tries to detour you off the path.

HELL

Satan is alive and well, roaming the earth. The Bible refers to him as the god of this age (2 Corinthians 4:4). But one day he will be thrown into the lake of fire, sometimes referred to as *hell*, (Revelation 20:10), and there he will spend eternity, along with all those who have rejected God's love and grace received through faith in Jesus Christ.

The Reality

Hell is a real place. Hell is not just an idea, or something we tell people so they will do what is right. The reality of hell is seen in Jesus' story about a rich man and a poor beggar named Lazarus (Luke 16:19-31). Both men represent two different lives. The rich man had all the comforts of this life, while Lazarus endured nothing but discomfort. Both men died, and then their lives switched roles. Because of his faith, Lazarus immediately entered the presence of Abraham (Luke 16:22), a Jewish term that describes a literal place of rest. Because of his lack of faith, the rich man ended up being tormented in hell (Luke 16:23).

From hell the rich man cried out for Abraham to send Lazarus to him with just a little cold water because the rich man said he was being afflicted with fire (Luke 16:24). Abraham reminded the rich man of the life he lived and the life Lazarus lived, and then told him that he could not send Lazarus, even if he wanted, because there was a huge chasm between them (Luke 16:25-26).

The rich man pleaded for Abraham to send Lazarus back from the dead, to his home, to warn his friends and family of the reality and horror of hell (Luke 16:27-28, 30). Abraham reminded the rich man that from the very beginning, through the prophets, people had been warned and even if someone rose from the dead, people still would not believe (Luke 16:29, 31)—an obvious prophecy of Jesus' own resurrection.

It may seem strange that Jesus chose this way to describe the reality of hell, but how else could He have done so? By telling this story, Jesus not only taught the reality of hell, He also taught that there is a conscious existence after death; one existence is torture, the other is comfort. Furthermore, He taught it was impossible for the dead to communicate with the living, and there is no second chance to respond to God's grace after death. What you choose to do with Jesus in this life makes a difference for eternity.

The Distinctions: Hades vs. Gehenna

In the Gospels, Jesus used two different words to describe hell.

The first word, the one used in the story of the rich man and Lazarus, was the word *Hades*. In Jesus' day, *Hades* could refer to the depths or the place of the dead. In certain contexts, like the one in Jesus' parable, *Hades* refers to hell, but it is not the final hell. *Hades,* however, should not be confused with *purgatory*.[3] *Hades* is a place of torture and the first place of punishment, but *Hades* is temporary. *Hades* is where the soul of a person who has rejected Jesus in this life goes to await the resurrection of all the dead, and the Great White Throne Judgment where the unbeliever will stand before God to give an account of his or her life (Revelation 20:11). *Hades* is where the rich man was. From *Hades* he was conscious of his own agony and the place of rest and comfort for Lazarus. Somehow, the rich man was also conscious of his friends and family whom he left behind, but he had no way of contacting them and warning them to stay away from *Hades*. While *Hades* is not eternal, it is excruciating. Once a person enters *Hades* there is no escaping their final destination.

The second word Jesus used to describe hell, and the one He used the most, was *Gehenna*. The word, *Gehenna*, has an interesting history. On the southern side of Jerusalem is a valley called the Valley of Hinnom (Joshua 15:8), which translates *Gehenna* in Greek. In the Old Testament, pagans used this valley to offer human sacrifices to the god Moloch (2 Chronicles 28:3; 33:6; 2 Kings 16:3). Later the Jews turned the valley into a city dump. All types of garbage and waste were thrown into the valley. The carcasses of dead animals were thrown into the pit, along with criminals and poor people who could not afford to be buried. A fire was constantly burning at the site to destroy the dead bodies and other refuse. Some of the dead bodies thrown into the valley would get stuck on the jagged rocks surrounding the valley. Wild animals and worms eventually devoured these bodies. When the wind blew in a certain direction, the smell of the valley would engulf parts of Jerusalem.

By using phrases like, "where the fire never ceases," "weeping and gnashing of teeth," and "worms devouring," (Matthew 8:11-12; Mark 9:43-48) to describe the horror of hell, Jesus used the worst earthly place to which His listeners could relate, the Valley of Hinnom, to describe the eternal punishment of hell. But the reality of hell is far worse than a valley on the south side of Jerusalem. Hell is real. Hell is literal. Hell is eternal. While *Hades* is temporary, *Gehenna* is forever. While *Hades* is only for the soul, *Gehenna* is for both body and soul. (See the chart, "Hades and Gehenna in the Gospels.")

HADES AND GEHENNA IN THE GOSPELS

Hades (appears 4 times in the Gospels)	*Gehenna* (appears 11 times in the Gospels)
Matthew 11:23 – Jesus denounces the cities where He performed miracles but people refused to repent. One of those cities, Capernaum, is cursed to *hades*.	Matthew 5:22 – Jesus teaches that a person who is angry with another person is guilty of murder and in danger of spending eternity in *gehenna*.
Matthew 16:18 – After Peter's confession that Jesus was the Christ (v. 16), Jesus says that the church will be built on Peter's confession and will be victorious, even over the gates of *hades*.	Matthew 5:29-30 – Jesus says that a person who lusts in his heart toward another person is guilty of adultery and in danger of spending eternity in *gehenna*.
Luke 10:15 – The same context and meaning as Matthew 11:23	Matthew 10:28 – Jesus explains that we should fear God more than people, because while people can kill the body, God can kill the body and soul in *gehenna*. The same thing is recorded by Luke in his gospel, Luke 12:5.
Luke 16:23 – Jesus' story of the rich man and Lazarus. Upon his death, the rich man's soul goes to *hades*, and from *hades* is in torment.	Matthew 23:15, 33 – Jesus condemns religious teachers as hypocrites and responsible for sending others to *gehenna*, and thus will not escape *gehenna* themselves.
SUMMARY: *Hades* is only for the soul and is temporary. *Gehenna* is for the body and the soul and is eternal. Both *hades* and *gehenna* are places of punishment and pain. Both *hades* and *gehenna* can be avoided by a person placing their faith in Jesus Christ.	Mark 9:43, 45, & 47 – Jesus explains that it is better to go through this life disabled and deformed than to spend eternity in *gehenna*, where worms do not die and the fire never goes out. A shorter version of this teaching by Jesus is found in Matthew 18:9

The End

Taking into account all that Scripture teaches, the following two scenarios summarize the events following a person's death.

Term for Christians: When you die, your body will return to the earth to wait for the resurrection. Your soul will immediately be in the presence of God, in a sort of temporary "heaven." At some point in the future, following the Second Coming of Christ, your dead body will be resurrected and reunited with your soul (John 5:28-29; 1 Thessalonians 4:14), in which you will stand before God. Your condemnation and penalty for sin was paid the moment you placed your faith in Jesus Christ; therefore, you will not stand before God guilty of sin, but to have your works for God evaluated for rewards (1 Corinthians 3:12-15). You will freely and exuberantly offer those rewards back to God in worship (Revelation 4:9). You will then enjoy eternity in the new heaven and new earth.

Non-Christ-followers: When they die, their bodies are buried to await the resurrection. Their souls immediately enter *Hades*, a sort of temporary hell. Following the Second Coming of Christ, the dead bodies of the non-Christ-followers will be resurrected and reunited with their souls (John 5:28-29), in which they will then stand before God at the Great White Throne Judgment (Revelation 20:11). Non-Christ-followers will give an account of their lives, and will be judged and found guilty because of their rejection of Jesus Christ. The punishment will be an eternity completely separated from the love and grace of God in *Gehenna*, the "lake of fire," the "second death" (Revelation 20:11-15).

The Necessity

The reality of hell illustrates both the holiness of God and the seriousness of sin. God is holy (Leviticus 19:2), which means *separate from sin*. You and I are sinful. Holiness and sin cannot coexist; sin must be punished by separation. If a holy, separate God did not punish sin, He would cease to be holy, and ultimately, He would cease to be God. Since God is eternal, and since all sin is ultimately against Him (Psalm 51:4), the punishment for sin is eternal separation from Him (Romans 6:23). The horror of hell is not the fire or the worms or the darkness or the torture. The horror of hell is that it will be an eternal, total separation from the holy love, holy grace, and holy forgiveness of God. Hell is a necessity because God is holy and our sins are serious.

What two real destinations are described in the Bible for where people will spend eternity after death?

_____

_____

Which is your current destination after you die, and how do you know this?

_____

_____

The Problem & Solution

The holiness of God explains the necessity of hell. But in reality, God doesn't send anyone to hell; people choose eternal separation from God through their rejection of Jesus Christ. Due to our sin, we *all* deserve hell. The question is not: Why does God send people to hell? The question is: Why does God allow anyone into heaven? God's immeasurable grace has offered salvation from hell to all who trust in Jesus as the payment for their sin.

Because Jesus is fully human He was able to die for your sins. Because Jesus is fully God, He had the power and perfection to die for your sins. By dying on the cross, Jesus, an eternal being, was able to pay the eternal penalty in a moment of time. When you, through faith, confessed Jesus as Lord and believed God raised Him from the dead (Romans 10:9-10), at that moment, Jesus' payment for sin became your payment for sin and you were adopted into the family of God. Through Jesus your sins have not just been forgiven, the eternal punishment for those sins has been paid in full, and you are no longer condemned (Romans 8:1).

Your response to hell should be to run to God. Your response to His forgiveness should be to tell others about God's love, grace, mercy, and forgiveness. What He has done for you, He will do for all who believe in Him.

Following Jesus is like going on a journey full of narrow twists and turns (Matthew 7:13-14). At times the path is perilous. At other times the scenery is breathtaking. Along this trail are detours and temptations that can lead to a dangerous eternity. Along this path hides a mortally wounded enemy that wants to ambush you and, like a wild animal, devour you (1 Peter 5:8). Don't be detoured. Pay close attention to the benchmarks along the way. Keep moving forward. Don't follow signs that lead to disappointment. Keep your bearings and stay on course. The path you are on leads to a glorious forever.

End Notes

[1] Ezekiel 28:1-19 is an interesting but complicated biblical passage to study. The passage is primarily about the king of Tyre. (This passage is similar to a description given of the king of Babylon in Isaiah 14:3-23.) While the biblical writer is describing a human

[2] It is important to note that in the Garden of Eden, Satan successfully used the same tactic of getting Adam and Eve to doubt what they knew to be true. Satan may be clever, but he is predictable.

[3] *Pergatory* (Latin, *purgare*, to make clean, to purify) is a place of temporary punishment in Catholic doctrine that certain people (mainly believers who have erred from truth) go to after death to be cleansed and purified. After the purifying process, the person is allowed into heaven. The doctrine of purgatory has been rejected by Protestant Christians because there is no biblical evidence of such a place.

chapter 9

Your Etiquette

David Trogdon

Just as no soldier should ever consider going to war alone, you, Christ-follower, should never consider walking through this life alone. Satan is the ultimate terrorist and a roaring lion so it would be foolish and dangerous to try to live for Jesus on your own. Christ followers need one another. Through faith you are all brothers and sisters in Jesus and members of the family of God. You must work together and walk with Jesus together if you are going to have any chance of spiritual victory and survival.

WALK TOGETHER LIKE JESUS YOUR LORD

You have probably seen the bumper sticker that reads, "Don't Follow Me. I'm Lost Too!" While following the wrong car on a highway may get you lost for a while, following the wrong leader may get you killed in combat or help cause you to become a spiritual casualty on the path to heaven. The road to heaven is not an easy or even a safe path. Satan is ready to attack at any moment. You must be sure you know where you are going each step of the way and exactly who you are following. The good news is that the Word of God presents you with His Son as your perfect example and guide for the Christian life and for your hike to heaven.

Instead of focusing on, following after, or comparing yourself to other Christ-followers, you must be sure to keep your eyes focused on Jesus continually. You must be sure you are following His Word and His example every step of the way so you can stay on the right path. You are to think like Jesus and do all you can to act like Him. Jesus is the ultimate model for Christian attitudes and actions. Jesus always loved, always submitted to His Father's will, always served others, and never thought of Himself. The heart, the head, and the hands of Jesus always perfectly obeyed and glorified God the Father.

Although you will never be totally like Jesus in this life, your ultimate goal must be to become more and more like Him. Being a Christ-follower is not just saying you believe in Jesus or going to church. Being a Christ-follower means you are committed to doing all you can to achieve this goal—to be like Jesus. That is what God expects of you as a Christ-follower and even what non-Christ-followers expect of you as well.

Read Philippians 2:1-10 and list all the attitudes and actions that should characterize the Christian life:

_____

_____

_____

In John 13:1-17, Jesus took on the role of a slave/servant and washed the disciples' dirty feet. What does our Lord's example in this passage teach us about the attitudes and actions required of a Christian servant (even to those who may need more washing than you)?

_____

_____

_____

How do you make sure others/non-Christians see that you are a Christ-follower by your attitude? Actions? And how you treat others? (John 13:35, 1 John 4:7-8)

_____

_____

Great leaders always lead by example. Jesus provided you with the perfect example, not only for living, but also for serving. Jesus, the very Son of God, humbled Himself, became an obedient servant to God the Father, and willingly laid down His life in place of yours on the cross. His example of sacrificial service should remind you that life is never about getting your own way or doing whatever you want, but always about loving and serving God and loving and serving others. If you continue to want your own way, seek to control everything, or want to receive the credit that only belongs to Jesus, then you are not walking on His path. A selfish, self-centered, proud Christ-follower is, in reality, following the path of this world's thinking instead of following the example and in the steps of Jesus. The thinking and wisdom of this world is totally contradictory to the thinking and wisdom of God (James 3:13-18). A genuine faith in Jesus always results in a changed life. Your life will demonstrate a desire to follow and please Jesus instead of self.

You are not walking alone on your way to heaven. You are walking together with fellow believers and fellow travelers. You share the same road. Having the mind of Jesus and following His example will result in your loving other Christ-followers and being committed to His Church. God commands all Christ followers to love one another, care about one another, encourage one another to remain faithful, and help one another when the road gets difficult.

Everyone will struggle. You should help those you see struggling and in turn others should help you when in similar situations. Having the mind of Jesus leads to you not enjoying or judging when others stumble or fall. Having the mind of Jesus also leads to never thinking yourself to be a better Christian when they do, but instead always standing ready to offer a hand to help them back up. Distancing yourself from the one who is struggling or has struggled does not provide needed help to a fellow Christ-follower nor does it resemble Jesus. In helping the fallen, you must be so careful not to stumble or fall yourself; however, leaving a friend down is not an option (Galatians 6:1-2). It is impossible to truly be committed to Jesus without also being committed to your fellow believers. You do not walk alone.

In Romans 12:1-2, in response to the sacrificial death of Jesus for our sins, what does the Bible call on you to do? According to the Free Will Baptist Church Covenant, what are you to do after you commit your life to Jesus, which serves as the basis for your "solemn covenant?"

_____

_____

What are your obligations to fellow Christ-followers? How do you respond to correction? (Covenant provided in the Appendix)

_____

_____

How did Jesus treat Peter in front of others after Peter's denial of being a Christ-follower? Read John 18:15-18, 25-27; 21:15-19.

_____

_____

While satanic attacks can be a difficult and painful time, the pain is much worse when you are hurt or "wounded" by those you love. Some Christ-followers do not share the path well. There are no Purple Hearts for "friendly fire" even though the wounds are just as real. The pain from a fellow Christ-follower can be more intense because the attack is unexpected coming from those who are supposed to love you.

One of the greatest tests of your spiritual maturity comes in how you respond when you are hurt or attacked by "friendly fire." It is at this moment when others, both those inside and outside the church, will see how much you are like Jesus. Do you make your fellow traveler your enemy? Do you hold grudges? Do you get even? Do you give up and drop out of church? Or, do you forgive like Jesus forgives?

No one has or will ever hurt you more than you have hurt and sinned against God. If Jesus can forgive you, then you can choose to forgive others no matter what they have done to you and no matter how badly you hurt.

Forgiveness is not forgetting but refusing to bring it up again to use against your offender. Romans 12:14-21 will help as you deal with difficult people. Forgiveness is never a feeling but always a choice to let go of the pain and a choice not to hurt others backing return. Forgiveness sets you free to live—free to love and free to keep walking with Jesus and one another.

In Matthew 6:14-15, what does Jesus say will happen if you forgive others? If you don't forgive others?

_____

_____

What is the basis for your forgiving others in Ephesians 4:32?

_____

_____

Is there someone you need to forgive? Someone you need to ask to forgive you?

_____

_____

_____

Soldiers know without much difficulty who is in charge and whose orders to follow. While the chain of command is clear in the military, sometimes Christians seem confused in the "army of God." The Word of God is very clear that Jesus is the Head of the Church. He is the One in charge and in control. Check the following Bible passages to see what God says about Jesus and His Church:

Read Matthew 16:18. Who owns your church and is ultimately responsible for church growth?

_____

_____

Read Colossians 1:18. In what areas should Jesus be in control in your church?

_____

_____

Walk Together in Christian Love

The journey to heaven is always much more enjoyable and easier when we walk together in love. The world has a warped and totally misguided view of love. Non-Christ followers often confuse love for a romantic feeling, infatuation, desire, pleasure, or even lust. "True love" cannot ever truly be found outside of a personal relationship with Jesus because "God is love" (1 John 4:16). Love is far more a commitment of your life to someone or to the wellbeing of another person than a feeling.

God's commitment to love you regardless of the pain you cause Him is a model for how you are to treat others on the journey. You can commit to love others only because God loves you. The more you enjoy the love of Jesus in your life, the more you can love others. The more you love others, the more you are willing to share the path in the way God intended.

The *family of God* is to be a loving community of believers in Jesus. A Christian church is successful in the eyes of God only as much as that church is loving. Numbers without a genuine love for Jesus and love for others do not impress God at all. Love is not optional for the Christian or for a church. God commands love. God never commands you to do anything that, through Jesus' enabling power, you cannot do. God loves you and desires joy for in your relationship with Him. Your relationship to God and your relationship to others is connected as seen in 1 John 4:7-21. You can make the choice to obey God's command and love others, even others who may seem hard to love at times. Because God chose to love you unconditionally, you can love one another unconditionally. It starts with a choice to love your fellow believers in Jesus, and a choice to love those who consider you their enemies.

What characteristics found in 1 Peter 3:8 should be visible in the lives of believers?

_____

_____

According to Jesus in John 13:34–35, what does your love prove to the world?

_____

_____

The Christian Church is made up of all kinds and types of people from every ethnic group, nationality, and personality, and all with different abilities and talents. Christians can be very different and yet all part of the same Church—the Body of Christ. Every believer or Christian has the same Lord, the same faith, the same Holy Spirit, the same mission, and they all walk on the same and only road to heaven together. What is it that enables so many who are so different to be of the same mind and mission? How can you keep unity in the midst of such diversity? The answer is found in the same love you have for Jesus and for one another. Love is the "glue" that holds the Church together. When your love fades, churches begin to experience trouble. Churches without love fall apart, split, and may even cease to exist. When your love falters, the Church suffers. When your love for Jesus and one another is fervent, the Church of Jesus Christ flourishes, the devil fails, and the Church grows together and goes forward together in unity.

Just as a body has many different body parts with different functions, there is still just one person. The Church of Jesus Christ is called the Body of Christ as well as the army of God and the family of God. These different names for the Church all reveal how that together in Jesus every Christ follower can have an amazing unity even with such great diversity. The key to that unity is the love of God that joins you together as one in Jesus.

The apostle Paul compares the Church to a body in 1 Corinthians 12:12–17. In what ways, is the church like a body?

_____

_____

Read about some of the spiritual gifts God gives Christians in Romans 12:3–10. What attitude, found in verse 3, should characterize your Christian service?

_____

What actions in verses 9-10 promote unity even with the diversity of spiritual gifts in the church?

_____

_____

Which Christian attitudes and actions promote peace and unity in the Body of Christ as listed in Ephesians 4:1-3?

_____

_____

According to the apostle Paul in 1 Corinthians 13, what is the most important attitude in the Church? How do you make that attitude evident for Jesus and His Church in your words and actions?

_____

_____

The unconditional love and grace Jesus intended for you to share will hold a church together and will grow a church closer together. As non-Christ-followers see Jesus' love lived out by Christ-followers in all relationships, they will be drawn to Jesus and to salvation. People are not attracted to Jesus by your church's programs or buildings, but by the Holy Spirit through your love! A loving church is a healthy church. Christians who walk together in love enjoy the journey far more and find others wanting to join them on the hike to heaven.

Walk Together in Christian Liberty

Freedom is not free. Your spiritual freedom came at a great price via the very blood of your Lord and Savior Jesus Christ. Jesus died for everyone so that whoever chooses Him could live in freedom and enjoy the journey to heaven.

The essence of freedom is being set free from the bondage of sin and being enabled to live with joy and to do what pleases God. Sin always enslaves; and your Savior can always set you free to serve Him.

In the Old Testament, God treated the children of Israel exactly like that—children. He gave them numerous detailed lists of what they could eat and not eat, what they could do and not do on the Sabbath, whom they could marry, what and how to plant their fields, and how to govern just about every area of life. These lists were necessary because, at that time, Israel did not have the indwelling Holy Spirit, the completed Word of God, or the assistance and guidance of a local church to help them stay on the right path.

In the New Testament and today, God trusts Christians to obey the clear commands and principles of Scripture, follow the guidance of the Holy Spirit, and listen to the advice of their spiritual leaders and other spiritually mature Christians on their path to heaven. God does not want you to follow someone else's man-made list of "dos and don'ts" in order to help you stay on the right path to heaven. Man-made lists bring bondage, confusion, trouble, and may even cause you to stray off the path of faith and freedom in Jesus.

There are several problems with following someone else's list. First, no two Christians are ever going to come to 100 percent agreement on every life choice of "dos and don'ts." Everyone's personal list will be different. Even committed and spiritually mature Christians do not agree on minor details and choices. Second, no list is going to be exhaustive and include every possible choice you must make. Finally, man-made lists can be used to control others or used to cause division or problems among genuine Christian brothers and sisters. This definitely is NOT the will of God!

Spiritual liberty is your freedom to make life choices according to the principles of Scripture and the guidance of the Holy Spirit who lives in you.

In Galatians 5:1, what is one reason that Jesus set you free and what does the apostle Paul warn you against?

_____

What does Paul warn you against in 1 Corinthians 8:9?

_____

_____

What one principle can help you make the right choices, according to Galatians 5:13-15?

_____

_____

Just as a husband and wife, who never agree 100 percent of the time but do not divorce over the minor differences of opinions, the same should be true of Christians. You will never agree 100 percent of the time on every life decision or even on every verse of Scripture. In those instances, you *agree to disagree.* Agreeing to disagree means that you can still love and get along with others while respecting their right to disagree with you.

Free Will Baptists strongly affirm everyone's right to be free to choose to receive Jesus and be saved and the freedom to reject Jesus and be lost. This personal freedom extends also to how you live and the choices each person makes. Free Will Baptists believe in *local church autonomy,* which is the right of every local church to own its own property and govern its own affairs. Local churches have joined together in associations, including the National Association of Free Will Baptists to encourage one another and to cooperate with each other to reach a lost world. Free Will Baptists (FWB) are committed to the Word of God as the ultimate and only authority. The FWB Church Covenant and *The Free Will Baptist Treatise of Faith and Practices* are embraced because it is understood that they accurately reflect the Word of God. Even though each Free Will Baptist is in the same denomination, follow the same Word of God and Free Will Baptist Treatise, each will still hold minor differences of opinions and disagreements with one another. In those instances, one must agree to disagree and keep on living for Jesus.

Read the "Articles of Faith" in the Free Will Baptist Treatise and answer the following questions:

What is the only "rule" for "faith or practice"? In other words, what is your infallible guide for all decisions and practices?

_____

What do Free Will Baptists believe about the "freedom of the will?"

_____

_____

How do you get along with Christ-followers from other denominations? Christ-followers from other denominations are just that—Christ-followers. You are all part of the same family of God. Different denominations agree, once again, on most of the Word of God and all the essentials of the faith and the Gospel. They disagree on some of the less important issues.

Free Will Baptists embrace different denominations who hold minor doctrinal distinctives. You can still walk together with Jesus even though you disagree at times on a few of the minor issues.

While genuine Christ-followers agree on most of the Word of God, what about those who claim to be following Jesus but who clearly do not follow God's Word? The Scriptures teach not to fellowship with those who claim to be Christ-followers, but reject the clear commands of the Word of God. The Bible also warns of the dangers of false religions and cults, that is, any group who denies the deity, person, and work of Jesus; reject the Bible as the only Word of God; and/or present different methods of salvation other than faith in Jesus. You cannot walk together with those who are going their own way and not following the Jesus of Scripture.

While some Christ-followers today seem to reject any denominational label, most often this is due to a misunderstanding of the nature and purpose of denominations. Denominations have several very positive purposes:

Denominations allow you to know what a church basically believes and how that church worships before you walk in the door.

Denominations join together to sponsor colleges, missionaries, publishing houses, etc., which very few churches could do with excellence on their own.

Denominations provide fellowship, leadership, and accountability to local churches even as individual Christ-followers do to one another.

Denominations allow Christ-followers to worship together with those who are like-minded in their understanding of doctrinal distinctives.

Even nondenominational churches fellowship, cooperate, and associate with other nondenominational churches and believers. These churches have a source for pastors, literature, missions, Christian education, etc. Imagine going to town in search of food, but none of the restaurants were identified by name on their signs. You wanted a certain type of and prefer certain food chains over others. You prefer to know what you will be eating or which chain you will be supporting with your business before going into the restaurant. In a similar way, denominational labels let you know the worship style and what distinctive beliefs a church holds before you go in to be "fed" by the Word of God.

You are to treat Christ-followers from other denominations just the same as you treat Christ-followers from your own. You are not to fight and argue over doctrine. You are not to look down on them, avoid them, or intentionally limit fellowship with them. Instead, you are to agree to disagree and recognize their spiritual liberty and freedom, and, if necessary, their *right to be wrong*. There may be times when Free Will Baptists can learn from other denominations while sharing the path and likewise these same denominations can learn from Free Will Baptists as well. You are to love them as your brothers and sisters in Jesus even though they may enjoy different styles of worship or may hold to different nonessential beliefs. You are sharing the same path and you are working for the same Son of God.

Read the following Bible passages. What kind of actions should cause you to not associate with a believer who claims to know Jesus but refuses to follow His Word?

Romans 16:17 _____

1 Corinthians 5:11 _____

2 Thessalonians 3:6 _____

What does your FWB Church Covenant have to say about the purpose of the FWB denomination?

_____

_____

What should your attitude be towards Christ-followers with whom you disagree, even those from other denominations?

_____

_____

Walking together and getting along with other Christ-followers can be difficult at times, especially those times when you may disagree. You can still walk together, agree to disagree, and use your spiritual liberty in love. You can even love and pray for those who are not walking according to the Word of God, even though you can't walk alongside them. Just as you are free to choose to walk with Jesus, according to His Word, they are free to choose not to do so.

In Luke 24:13-35, Jesus, shortly after His resurrection from the dead, walked along and talked with two of His disciples while on the road to Emmaus. The hearts of His disciples "burned within them" as their Lord walked together with them. Jesus has given you the "gift" of Himself and the wonderful privilege of being adopted into His family. He wants to walk with you and for you to enjoy His presence as you live for Him. He also desires that Christ-followers, as fellow laborers and fellow citizens of His Kingdom, walk together with Him on the road to Heaven. From this day forward, make sure that every step you take on this path to heaven is a step together with Jesus and with His Church!

Examine Romans 14:1—15:7 and list the numerous principles you find concerning how to exercise your spiritual liberty:

_____

_____

Consider these questions when deciding if a choice is a wise or unwise:

• What does the Bible say about this? If the Bible clearly forbids it, then there is no reason to even consider it.

• Will this action bring glory to God?

• Could it be considered holy and righteous (a right thing to do) or could it be considered unholy and wrong?

• Will my doing this help or hinder my journey and fellowship with Jesus?

• Will this action damage my Christian witness? Will non-Christ-followers use this as a reason or an excuse not to follow Jesus?

• Is it possible for this action to lead me into bondage or addiction?

• Could my doing this cause another Christian to be hurt or fall into sin?

Your Itinerary

STEWARDSHIP

You are a Christian, a Christ-follower, or a believer. Whatever title you use for having asked for forgiveness and inviting Jesus to be the center of your life, you now face a new direction in life. You are continuing the journey—your spiritual hike. The destination is spiritual maturity, which will ultimately be reached when you are in heaven, but you will gain more and more maturity in Christ with every step following Him as your Guide.

As with any trip, this hike has an itinerary, or proposed route of travel for the trip. You might think of the itinerary as the management of your trip. Growing spiritually will require some management. The biblical word for management is *stewardship*, and the Bible teaches there are certain things of which you must be a good steward. One is your spiritual gift(s). Another is your resources, primarily your time and money. You must also be a good steward of your commitments to your church.

The Stewardship of Your Spiritual Gifts

The stewardship of spiritual gifts involves three things. The first is defining spiritual gifts. The second is discovering your specific spiritual gift or gifts. The third is deciding to use your spiritual gifts in your church.

Defining Spiritual Gifts

What are spiritual gifts? A spiritual gift is a God-given ability that enables a Christ-follower to effectively serve others. God, through the Holy Spirit, is your Guide and the Giver of spiritual gifts and abilities (1 Corinthians 12:4-11). God determines spiritual gifts; you do not choose or earn them. Since the purpose and intent of gifts are to enable you to effectively serve others, it is important that you discover and use your unique gifts.

Romans 12, 1 Corinthians 12, and Ephesians 4 are the three primary chapters in the New Testament that list spiritual gifts. None of these three lists is exclusively exhaustive. Some of the gifts are mentioned several times. Some are mentioned only once. Some you find in other places in Scripture isolated apart from a list. The spiritual gifts listed in these three passages are all referred to as gifts of the Holy Spirit. First Corinthians 12:4 states there are different kinds of gifts, but the same Spirit is the Source of all the gifts.

There appear to be three different types of gifts. First, there are **office** gifts. These gifts are given to people for serving in a specific office or position in the church, such as apostle, prophet, evangelist, or pastor-teacher (Ephesians 4:11-12). The offices of apostle and prophet no longer exist and only evangelist and pastor-teacher gifts remain now that the foundation of the church has been laid (Ephesians 2:19-22).

Second, there are **service** gifts. These are gifts in areas of ministry that every Christ-follower is expected to participate. However, some people are given a spiritual gift to equip them for greater impact for ministry in certain areas. For example, all Christ-followers are expected to share their faith with others, but some have the spiritual gift of evangelism. They are especially effective in sharing their faith as well as leading others to do so.

Third, there are **sign** gifts. These are listed in 1 Corinthians 12:9b-10. These gifts were given to the early church during the first century as a fulfillment of Old Testament prophecy (1 Corinthians 14:21) and a sign of confirmation that Messiah had appeared (Acts 2:16-18). Some see these as continuing today. However, just as God no longer speaks through direct revelation inspiring additional books of the Bible, many Christ-followers, including Free Will Baptists, believe that sign gifts have fulfilled their intended purpose and therefore have ceased. The temporary nature of certain gifts is indicated in 1 Corinthians 13:8.

These are the gifts primarily named in 1 Corinthians 14:4-12. Other Christ-followers believe that all the spiritual gifts named in the Bible continue today. However, just as God does not continue to speak through direct inspiration resulting in additional books of the Bible today, the sign gifts also have served their original purpose for a specific period of time (1 Corinthians 14:21-22).

Discovering Your Spiritual Gift(s)

As important as it is to know *about* spiritual gifts, it is even more important to understand which spiritual gifts *you* uniquely possess. To discover your spiritual gifts, you need to first answer these four questions: Who receives spiritual gifts? When are spiritual gifts given? Why are spiritual gifts given? How are spiritual gifts identified once received?

Who receives spiritual gifts? While there is some disagreement about the total number of spiritual gifts available, the Bible is quite clear that *every* Christ-follower receives at least one spiritual gift (1 Corinthians 12:4-11; 1 Peter 4:10-11). If you have been forgiven of your sins by Jesus' death on the cross and resurrection—that is, if you are a Christian—then you have received at least one spiritual gift, and you may quite possibly possess more than one.

When are spiritual gifts given? Since the Bible teaches that every Christ-follower has received a least one spiritual gift, it seems that spiritual gifts are given when a person accepts Jesus as Savior. You received your natural talents by virtue of your birth into your biological family. Similarly, you received your spiritual gifts as part of your spiritual birth into the family of God. Sometimes your natural talents work hand in hand with your spiritual gifts.

Why are spiritual gifts given? The purpose of spiritual gifts is to enable Christ-followers to effectively serve the greater body of Christ, which consists of the people of His Church (Romans 12:4-8). The local church and the church at large both function like a body. Every part of the body has a particular role and function and is important to the health of the whole person. Your spiritual gifts are given to you to enable you to fulfill your God-given role in the body of Christ. This is why there are so many different gifts. As a Christ-follower, you need the church, and your church needs you.

Name some spiritual gifts you see in your pastor.

_____

_____

What would happen if people in church chose not to use their spiritual gifts?

_____

_____

How are spiritual gifts identified? Taking a *spiritual gifts assessment* or inventory can be very helpful in assisting you to understand and identify your unique spiritual gifts. These assessments offer explanations of the various spiritual gifts, and seek to connect key observable qualities or characteristics in your spiritual life with one or several of these gifts as seen in Scripture. Along with taking a spiritual gifts inventory, there are a few other important things you should do to identify your gifts.

Study what the Bible teaches about spiritual gifts. Dig into passages like Romans 12, 1 Corinthians 12, and Ephesians 4, and then note how characters in the Bible use their spiritual gifts throughout the book of Acts and the remainder of the New Testament. Also, **watch** how other Christ-followers in your church use their spiritual gifts.

Pray and ask God to show you what spiritual gifts He has given you. Remember, He wants you to discover your gifts, and to use them.

Ask other Christ-followers who know you well to tell you what spiritual gifts they think you have. They may have seen evidence of a spiritual gift in your life that you never even considered.

You should consider completing the spiritual gifts assessment now, and then again a year from now to observe any development of your understanding of your gifts. Repeating this process every two years will help you confirm that you are on the right track. Remember this spiritual gift assessment is *not* a test and there is no pass or fail. It is simply an inventory tool for identifying what gifts you currently possess.

Start serving by getting involved in some of the ministries of your church. By volunteering to help out in a variety of areas you can discover the place that fits who you are. While this may sound like a process of *trial and error* it is really discovering your spiritual gifts by *trial and correction.*

Using Your Spiritual Gifts

Two very important things happen when you discover and use your spiritual gifts. The first is that you clarify God's will for your life. When you discover your gifts and begin to use them, you are fulfilling His purpose for you.

The second is that the entire church benefits. The purpose of spiritual gifts is to benefit the body of Christ. No one will benefit if you keep your spiritual gifts hidden. You will lose the benefit of seeing the Holy Spirit at work in your life, your church will lose out on what the Holy Spirit can do for others through you, and most important, God is not glorified (1 Peter 4:10-11).

A church is strong and healthy only when it is filled with people who use their spiritual gifts to serve others (1 Timothy 4:14; 2 Timothy 1:6). Notice how you are benefiting from others who use their spiritual gifts through teaching, singing, ushering, greeting, serving, and other ministries. You can be the recipient of another's gift, or you can be the giver, providing blessings and help to others. Do not solely be a taker; be a giver as well.

Spiritual Gifts Analysis

(available at www.churchgrowth.org)

The web site provides you with an easy thorough online assessment of the your spiritual gifts. Free Will Baptist did not write this assessment but this tool provides more thorough description of various gifts than other traditional assessments providing only seven or nine gifts. However the gifts of healing, apostle, and prophet needs your pastor to provide a better definition than this instrument provides. Free Will Baptist will not agree with how these are interpreted. That being said, the assessment is free, thorough, self-scoring and one of the most helpful spiritual gifts inventories you will find. Remember there are no right or wrong answers, just answers that help reveal your strengths.

Then provide some fill in the blanks for them to transfer the results

Dominant Gifts   Sub-Dominant Gifts

_____   _____

_____   _____

_____   _____

_____   _____

Help Your Children or Grandchildren Discover Their Spiritual Gifts

Every Christ-follower, including children who follow Jesus, possesses at least one spiritual gift. Spiritual gifts are faith-based and not age-based. The presence of gifts in children should not be overlooked, and parents should provide opportunities that allow children to use and develop their gifts. Development occurs by using the gift and learning from others with similar gifts. Children discover and develop their spiritual gifts the same way adults do. However, they do need age-appropriate opportunities.

For example, a spiritual gifts assessment may not be very helpful for children due to their life development and experience. But you can teach children about the church and spiritual gifts in a way they understand. You can pray for and with your children that God will show them what gifts He has given them.

No one knows your children better than you. Watch for their gifts and talents by encouraging their development through affirming words and encouraging opportunities to use them. As you observe their lives, you are in a very unique position to see what gifts they may possess. No one will be as effective as you in helping them to develop that gift.

Children need opportunities to serve in the church. As children develop experience in ministry, they can also begin to identify how they may be gifted. Serving together as a family is a great way for both you and your children to discover and develop your spiritual gifts.

So identify your spiritual gifts, then start using and developing them. Be a good steward, or manager, of your gifting by serving others.

THE STEWARDSHIP OF YOUR RESOURCES

Many people mistakenly think that stewardship applies only to money. However, *stewardship* is a much broader term. God wants you to be a trustworthy steward, or manager, of *all* the resources He has given to you, including your time and talents. As a genuine Christ-follower, you must acknowledge that God really owns everything (Psalm 24:1) and you are following Him as your Guide. This means giving up claim to ownership of all that you have. It requires nothing less than a whole new way of thinking and living. It's not just the world that belongs to God. *You* belong to God too. God owns everything. He adopted you, and you chose to call Him Father.

A steward is a manager of someone else's possessions. God owns and you manage. Your responsibility is to be faithful with what God has entrusted to you. Faithfulness simply means putting God first. There are three things you can do to put God first in your life.

Give God the First Thoughts of Every Day

While you can spend time with God most any time of the day, many great men and women serving God give Him an appointment early in the day. Give God the first thoughts of every day (Psalm 5:3). Take the time to pray and read God's Word every day. When you have given Him your first thoughts, your remaining thoughts will be more easily directed the correct way as well.

Give God the First Day of Every Week

Second, give God the first day of every week. Ever since the resurrection of Jesus Christ on the first day of the week, His followers have traditionally worshiped Him on Sunday. Although it is not the specific day of the week that is important (Romans 14:5), it is important that you *do* worship with other believers (Hebrews 10:24-25). Be part of the church and give God time that is focused on Him.

Give God the First 10 Percent

Third, give God the first 10 percent of every paycheck. This is called *tithing*. Honoring God with your finances is an important part of your Christian walk. You might be surprised to know there is more written in the Bible about money than any subject other than God Himself. One reason for this is that money competes with God for first place in your life. Many people make money their top priority. Jesus said that you must choose to serve one of these two masters (Matthew 6:24). He said you cannot serve both God and money. Money can be a rival god. It is interesting that Jesus said your heart will be where your treasure is, and not that your treasure will be where your heart is (Luke 12:34).

Another reason for the prominence of money in the Bible is that so much of your life revolves around the use of money. Think about how much time you spend each week earning money, deciding how to spend money, saving money, or even just worrying about money. Money has a huge influence on your life. God loves you too much *not* to say something about money. Knowing and obeying God's financial principles will be critical to your success on your journey to spiritual maturity.

What is tithing? The word *tithe* means *one tenth*. For Christ-followers, tithing is giving 10 percent of their income back to God. Tithing was *commanded* in the Old Testament. It is *commended* by Jesus in the New Testament (Matthew 23:23). While the New Testament does not teach that you are to give specifically ten percent, it does teach that you are to give in proportion to your material blessings and emphasizes sacrificial giving (1 Corinthians 16; 2 Corinthians 9). This means the standard for giving is higher in the New Testament, not lower than in the Old Testament. Tithing should be the minimum for your giving, not the maximum. What was once a command is now a model, and what was once a percentage in now a proportion.

There are two extremes of which to be aware and avoid regarding tithing. One is the danger of legalistically giving 10 percent, and then thinking that the remaining 90 percent is yours to save or spend as you like. Remember, God owns everything and as you learned earlier in this chapter, God is the Source or Giver of all things and you are to be a responsible steward of 100 percent of what God has given you. The other extreme is thinking since the New Testament does not give a set standard for giving, you can give whatever you want.

Why should you tithe? God has a purpose for tithing. One purpose of tithing is that it teaches God's people to put Him first in everything (Deuteronomy 14:22-23). Another purpose for giving the tithe is to provide for the financial needs of the church.

God does not command you to give because He needs your money. The truth is that God does not need anything from you at all (Psalm 50:9-12). Giving is what God tells you to do to break the spiritual power money has over you. Tithing is acknowledging that everything you have is God's, and it demonstrates your willingness to steward your resources for His purposes. It reminds you to manage well all that God has given you.

Giving to God is also an act of worship (Psalm 96:8-9). It acknowledges His authority over us and our dependence on Him. It is an appropriate expression of thanksgiving for all He has provided.

How should you tithe? Throughout Scripture, your first priority is a portion of what you bring home belongs to God. The Old Testament identifies ten percent as the base tithe; there were various other offerings as well. (Interestingly, Jesus typically challenged His followers to a higher standard [Matthew 5:21-44]).

There is also a designated place to give. In the Old Testament, God's people brought their tithes to the storehouse, which was a reference to the Temple (Malachi 3:10). The tithe was brought to the place where the people worshiped. Today, that is your church. Your tithe should be given to your church.

More important than the amount you give is your attitude in giving it. An attitude of love in giving is crucial (1 Corinthians 13:3). If giving is merely to a church, a ministry, or a needy person, it is only charity. But giving becomes an act of worship when it is given to the Lord (Numbers 18:24). When the offering plate is passed at your church, remind yourself that you are giving to the Lord Himself.

We are also to give cheerfully (2 Corinthians 9:7). God loves a cheerful giver. The word *cheerful* literally means hilarious. How can we be hilarious givers? The key to this kind of attitude in giving is to submit yourself to Jesus and ask Him to direct how much He wants you to give (2 Corinthians 8:1-5). Then you can experience the blessing of giving with the proper attitude.

What happens when you tithe? God never intended tithing to be a burden on you but instead a blessing. You are probably wondering how in the world you can reduce your available income by 10 percent and still get by financially. If you are faithful to God in your giving, regardless of your financial situation, He will be faithful in taking care of you (Malachi 3:8-10).

If you wait until you think you are financially able to tithe, you will never do it. There will always be another thing to buy or pay off. If you never tithe, you will miss out on the blessings that come from trusting God and supporting His work.

How do you receive spiritual gifts and financial resources?

_____

_____

How is tithing and giving offerings similar to using your spiritual gifts in the church?

_____

_____

Describe how using your gifts and tithing is a form of worship toward God?

_____

_____

The Stewardship of Your Commitments

You probably have heard of *covenants.* The practice of covenant-making has existed for centuries. Very simply, a covenant establishes a contractual relationship that did not naturally or normally exist. For example, you may have a homeowners' association covenant where you live. You agreed to that covenant when you moved into your neighborhood, and you now have a relationship with all the other people who live in that neighborhood. There are certain stipulations in the covenant you agree to uphold as a resident of that neighborhood. Marriage is a covenant. When a man and woman get married, they are making a covenant to live together as husband and wife for the rest of their lives. Covenants in ancient times would be agreed upon by two kings or between a king and his subjects. God even established covenants with His people because He desired a unique relationship with them.

It is important that you join a church as a Christ-follower. It is the way God intended for you to grow in your faith. Free Will Baptists have adopted a church covenant, and this covenant outlines several commitments, stipulations, or guidelines that members of a Free Will Baptist church agree to uphold.

Stewardship of Your Reputation

As a Christ-follower, you now represent Jesus and His Church. You are even called an ambassador of Christ (2 Corinthians 5:20). This is why the first promise you make in the covenant is to protect your reputation. What people think about you is also what they think about Jesus and

His Church (Proverbs 22:1). There are some behaviors and attitudes you will now embrace, and some you will now avoid because you are a Christ-follower.

Stewardship of Your Spiritual Growth

Your covenant calls for a commitment to spiritual growth. You grow spiritually through worship, prayer, Bible study, sharing your faith, giving, and serving in the church. The covenant rightly acknowledges the importance of these activities by saying they are not optional, but calls them *obligations.*

Stewardship of Your Church

As a Christ-follower, you have the privilege and responsibility to be involved in the life of your church. A Christ-follower without a church family is an orphan. Your covenant calls you to faithfully attend the services of your local church, to observe the ordinances, and to financially support the ministry of your church.

Stewardship of Your Relationships

One of the most important commitments you make in your covenant is the commitment to protect the unity of the church. Relationships are vital to a church. You must value, care for, and protect each other. Just as your reputation is important, you are to watch and protect other Christ-followers' reputations. Humility is the key to healthy relationships in the church. Pride will destroy the unity and witness of a church. Knowing relationships are vital to the body of Christ or His Church.

Stewardship of Kingdom Growth

The goal of every Christ-follower and local church should be, as the Free Will Baptist covenant states, "to extend the influence of Christ." Jesus gave His followers a Great Commission (Acts 1:8). You are to contribute to His witness—whether physically, financially, or prayerfully—in every part of the entire world.

How can you use your gifts and be part of what God wants to do now? (Matthew 6:10).

_____

_____

God trusts you to manage all He has given to you. What areas do you need to manage better?

_____

_____

CONCLUSION

Now that you have received the itinerary for your hike toward spiritual maturity, will you make the commitment to be a good steward? Stewardship of your spiritual gifts, resources, and commitments to your church are vitally important to your successful spiritual growth. Steward well, and go grow.

chapter 11

Your Responsibility

David Potete & Gowdy Cannon

FRUIT ON THE PATH: EVIDENCE YOU'RE FOLLOWING JESUS

Every year, national park rangers spend a significant amount of their time searching on the main trails and off the trails looking for lost or injured hikers. Hikers, unknowingly, follow the wrong trail taking them far from the intended destination often times without them knowing how to make it back on their own. Experienced hikers have an obligation to help other hikers on the journey. You should share equipment insights, trail challenges, and encourage healthy habits. Every responsible hiker looks for and helps find lost hikers before the elements cause great or permanent harm. As Christ followers, this study has prepared you for the journey of a lifetime but that does not mean it will be easy for you or for those around you. What do you do about other Christ followers who are losing their way? You should look for other hikers who have never been introduced to the Guide, God Who through the Holy Spirit, Jesus Christ, and the Father comprise one God willing and capable of leading any who will follow.

One of the most profound aspects of the gospel is that the condition for salvation is faith. *Faith* is more than "I believe there is a God." James 2:14-26 explains that faith is *belief in action*. Note this does not mean you are saved by your works, but instead that a faith which does not produce works is not true faith. Notice as well James says that even the demons believe in God (and fear Him), affirming that mere belief and head knowledge is not true faith. Earlier James writes that you are not just to hear the Word of God preached, but to actually do it or put it into practice (James 1:22). Attending Bible studies and listening to sermons in worship services are important to spiritual health, but these things are meaningless if you do not put into practice what you hear. Jesus agrees with this in Matthew 7:24-27 by saying anyone who hears His words and does not put them into practice is like a foolish man with a house on the sand. Those who do put them into practice are like a wise man with a house on the rock.

In other places the Bible continues to confirm this principle. For example, seeing someone in need and not helping him or her is evidence you do not have the love of God (1 John 3:17). Then later the Bible connects this to salvation by saying that a person who does not love is not a true Christ-follower (1 John 4:8). Proverbs 3:27-28 is the Old Testament version of 1 John 3:17.

There is no doubt that a person becomes a Christian or Christ-follower entirely by grace through faith (Ephesians 2:8-10). Faith is not obtained by anything you do. However, faith results in doing and living out, and not just having or possessing. We do what we do as Christ-followers not to earn grace; rather we do these things because *we have already received grace!* We live for God and for others out of a heart of gratitude.

You should be able to tell a difference between people who are or are not Christ-followers by how they live their lives, and this is not limited to just how they react to people in need. Galatians 5:19-23 even gives two lists of evidences, or fruit, one for the person who is not a Christ-follower, and the other for the person who is a follower of Jesus Christ. Things like *goodness, faithfulness,* and *peace* define the Christ-follower, while words like *selfish ambitions, envy,* and *drunkenness* describe the person who is not following Jesus.

Jesus used the terminology of *fruit* numerous times to mean evidence of following Him (Matthew 3:8-10; 7:15-20; 21:43). However, be careful that you do not become prideful in your efforts. The Bible reminds that you can do no good without Jesus, as He taught in John 15:1-9. Jesus also taught in Luke 17:7-10 that when you do what is right, you are only following the basic commands expected of a servant, and are not accomplishing anything extraordinary from your heart. Self-righteousness is a problem all Christ-followers must recognize. The Bible describes the *fruit* coming from the Spirit of God, and not from your good intentions.

Gowdy's father was a shining example of this. He is not a pastor or missionary, and he has never held any major leadership position in any church. However, he has taught the same Sunday School class for the past 40 years. He has farmed the same soil for the past 50 years. He gave up a college education and his dream of being a history professor to come back to the farm because his father was an alcoholic and could not run the farm any longer. Most important, Gowdy's father demonstrated faithfulness in how he raised five children to follow Jesus. Three of them are not his biological children, yet they all call him "Daddy." He constantly taught his children about God and the Bible, not only with his words, but even more so with his life, actions, and even his attitude. Oftentimes Gowdy says, "my dad taught me ___" and referring to something he did not say, but lived. The world would not consider my father "great" or his accomplishments amazing; however, if living by faith is the standard, Gowdy's father is a great man of God.

Look for people who live what they say, and do not just go through the motions. The genuineness speaks far louder than words or claims. You should strive to let your actions and attitudes reflect Jesus, and your words will certainly follow.

List people who you know who may not be following Christ. (Start praying now for an opportunity to share about your new path with them).

_____

_____

Read Ephesians 2:8-10 and list what you can do to earn becoming a Christ-follower, earn salvation or merit Heaven. (Your list should be blank)

Read Galatians 5:19-23 and list areas to improve.

_____

_____

U-TURNS: QUITTING IS NOT AN OPTION

The flip side of Christ-followers *living by faith* is when individuals fall into living by their natural desires to do wrong and thus provide evidence of a *lack of faith*. If you follow your pre-Jesus natural tendencies, you can be led away from your relationship with Him. For example, you will notice in the Bible a spectrum related to the Christ-follower distancing him or herself from God. Included in this spectrum is what many call *backsliding*, during which a Christ-follower drifts back into his or her former lifestyle and stops consistently manifesting the fruit of the Spirit. While this straying from God is most certainly described in the Bible, we should note that the word *backsliding* itself is rarely used. What is not rare, however, are illustrations of this backsliding. In fact, the whole story of Israel in the Old Testament is one of God's people following the Lord and then drifting away.

The Bible describes Israel's backsliding using various terms, such as *rebelling* (Isaiah 1:2, 5), *continuing to sin* (Psalm 78:17, 32), and *doing evil* (Jeremiah 52:2-3). Whatever you call it, the Jews were prone to wander, and at the heart of their waywardness, as is true with all sin, was unbelief, distrust, and disobedience (Psalm 78:7, 22, 32). God is not one, however, to allow man's sin to shut down His efforts to reclaim wandering man. In a great display of mercy, God punished the Jews in an effort to bring them to their senses and back to Him. The result frequently was that they *did* return to the Lord, and He showed them undeserved grace and mercy by forgiving them (Ezekiel 16:59-63).

The same picture of waywardness can be seen in the New Testament. For example, Paul wrote 1 Corinthians to a Christian church involved in many different sins. In this letter, he corrected these wandering believers and urged them to turn back to God and to begin again producing the fruit of the Spirit. Thus, in both the Old and New Testaments, you see examples of people being forgiven for the sin of *backsliding*.

The Bible also speaks, however, of the possibility of Christ-followers renouncing their faith and ultimately ceasing to be Christians. In Hebrews 3:12, the writer pointedly indicates to a group of Christ-followers that they are not to have a sinful, unbelieving heart that turns them away from the living God. He gives clear warning that unbelief is not a minor issue but one that can terminate one's relationship with God. Later, in Hebrews 6:4-6, the same writer explains that once individuals who have become Christ-followers turn away into unbelief, they will be unable to return to following Jesus once again.[1] You can't get more serious than that.

This is a hard teaching, but the idea seems to be that just as faith is what connects people to Jesus, so rejection—or giving up—of faith removes people from a relationship with Him. Further, there is a certain finality to the words of Hebrews 6, which indicates that those described can no longer return to a relationship to God after they have renounced their faith. As Hebrews 6:4 says, it is impossible for them to do so.

Many conclude from this terrible description of apostasy that Christ-followers who have eternally renounced their spiritual family ties will not even desire to return to God because they have avoided and shielded themselves from the conviction of the Holy Spirit for so long that He has ceased to draw them to repentance. Clearly we are not dealing here with an isolated fall into sin. These verses are describing an attitudinal shift from belief in Christ to unbelief.

Some people call this *apostasy* and others call it *losing* faith. This latter expression is not strictly accurate, since the Bible makes it clear that apostate individuals *choose* this outcome. They don't *lose* their faith but rather *voluntarily* forfeit their relationship with Jesus. In other words, it does not happen by accident.

Does this mean that individual sins are nothing to worry about? Absolutely not! For while no single fall into sin need cause Christ-followers to forfeit their faith, consistent sin may very well lead to abandoning the Lord. Think of it this way. In a sense, all sin is an expression of unbelief, and so the danger is that these individual momentary faith failures may lead to a general disposition of faithlessness. In this regard, it is helpful to see apostasy as a culminating event, resulting from a process of wandering. In the same way that one becomes a Christian by making a willful, conscious decision to follow Jesus by faith, so one becomes an apostate by making an equivalent willful, conscious decision to leave their faith. You can see that both of these decisions, to follow God or to leave Him, may come as the culmination of a lengthy process.

This teaching fits well with man's original design. God created humanity as *free moral agents* with the ability to choose to obey or disobey. This freedom clearly was in place in the Garden of Eden. It seems that God made freedom an essential part of mankind's makeup. If so, this truth has major implications for man's spiritual standing. For example, the Lord does not remove a person's freedom to choose after he becomes a Christ-follower. The freedom he had to accept Jesus is the same freedom he has to choose no longer to follow Him. A person does not cease to be free simply because he has trusted Christ.

We should note that this action of Christ-followers forfeiting their faith is *not* something to be expected (Hebrews 6:9). Such an abandonment of God after the acknowledgment and acceptance of His grace would be totally contrary to the work of God in that person's life (Philippians 1:6). Through His Holy Spirit, God convicts and strengthens and encourages and forgives and provides all things necessary for the life of faith. No dark spiritual force can pry us away from faith in God, so there is no need for a Christ-follower to live in fear of being overcome by the devil. The Lord promises us clearly that nothing outside our own volition can take us out of a relationship with Him and that He will always be faithful to us no matter what we do (John

10:27-30; Romans 8:35-39). Satan, his demons, and all other humans are powerless in affecting our faith and our standing with God. If God be for us, we need not fear. We need only follow.

When did freedom of choice or will begin in the Bible? When did freedom of will begin in your life and when will it end?

_____

_____

In the rare times this occurs, does a person lose his or her salvation or does he or she choose to give it up?

_____

_____

Describe "backsliding" as mentioned above. Tell about the dangers and what precautions you can take to avoid backsliding (Give at least one Scripture to show this).

_____

_____

Additional Notes:

For specific examples of apostates, though they are not named, we should perhaps reference in place of these names the individuals mentioned in 1 Timothy 4:1-6, 1 Timothy 6:9-10, 20-21, and 2 Peter 2:18-22, who not only have "wandered away from the faith," "gone astray from the faith," "fell away from the faith" and become "again entangled in the world," but also sought to bring others with them.

RESCUING OTHER HIKERS: SHARE YOUR STORY

Imagine if on a hike you see people headed in the wrong direction, far off the trail. You call out to them and they respond, crying out with relief. "We are lost", they cry. Imagine your joy at being able to point them to the path that will take them safely home. As a hiker, you want to rescue anyone who is lost and off the trail.

In the same way, one of the greatest joys of being a follower of Christ is to lead someone who is lost to the Savior. Having found eternal life and a vibrant relationship with Christ through faith in Him, you have the privilege and responsibility to share with others how they, too, can come to know Him.

Just as a hiker would be alert to other hikers who are in trouble, you can be alert to opportunities to tell others about the Savior who found and rescued you. Begin each day anticipating divine appointments in which God brings someone across your trail who is lost and needing a Savior. Pray for those opportunities, and for guidance in how to share the good news about Jesus. As you look for opportunities, keep the following rules of the trail in mind:

• *Following Christ is about more than a mere decision; it is about a lifelong relationship.* Rather than pushing someone to make a decision based on momentary emotion, we should aim for long-term faith. Help those with whom you share understand that receiving Christ is the beginning of a growing relationship with a living Savior who desires to walk with them and guide them through life.

• *Salvation is a supernatural process.* Our job is not to twist people's arms, rushing them into a decision they are not ready for. It is the work of the Holy Spirit to convict and convince people of the truth. They have to come to Christ of their own free will, having been drawn to trust Him by the work of the Spirit in their hearts.

• *Don't confuse sanctification with salvation.* We should not expect those who don't yet know Christ to behave like those who do. Holiness follows salvation; it doesn't precede it.

• *Keep it simple.* Being born again is not complicated. Here's a simple way to explain how a person can begin a relationship with Christ:

Acknowledge your need of a savior (Romans 3:10, 23).

Confess your sins (Romans 10:13, 1 John 1:9).

Trust in Christ's sacrifice for your sins and His resurrection (Romans 10:9-10).

Surrender your life to God's transforming power (Romans 12:1-2).

Just as you would study a map and memorize the route and terrain for a hike, you can memorize these (and other) verses and prepare yourself to explain how to be born again. You don't have to be a Bible expert, but you will be more and more effective in your witness, and in following Christ, as you study and memorize God's word.

Be ready to share how you came to make your decision to trust and follow Christ. Be ready to explain what your life was like before you came to Christ. Share what brought you to the point of deciding to trust Christ. And finally, share the difference knowing and following Christ has made in your life. You might want to put these things on paper in order to rehearse how best to share them simply and concisely. And remember, your job is simply to point people to the One who can guide them safely home.

Pause and write down a little of what it was like for you before Christ. What led to your decision to follow Christ and what it has done as you follow Him today?

_____

_____

Now find someone (friend, classmate) to share your story. Try to do this in three minutes or less. Then ask them if you can share how one finds a relation with Christ and walk them through the ACTS plan above. (You might write this in the front of your Bible)

SUPPORT THE TEAM: SHARING ACROSS THE GLOBE

Read Haggai 1:1-15. In the context, God wanted His people to build a temple for worship, similar to a church building and the people were apathetic. They lived in paneled houses, which meant they spent money to make their houses extra comfortable, while the temple remained in ruins. Twice God told them to give careful thought to their ways (1:5, 7).

In the current-day context, God desires His followers to build churches of *people*, not *buildings*. Yet, Christ-followers often approach their faith living in paneled houses, becoming arrogant, and being overfed and unconcerned with the needs of others (Ezekiel 16:49).

The words God spoke to Israel several thousand years ago about their temple is appropriate for all Christ-followers to apply today to churches built of people. Considering your ways will lead to making wise decisions which help advance God's kingdom. Self-evaluation is a biblical principal.

There are several ways in which you can invest time and money to build God's church not only in your hometown, but also around the world. Free Will Baptists have both North American missionaries and international missionaries who reach people for Jesus all over the world. Missionaries are located in places like Brazil, France, and Japan, and many other countries where less than one percent of the population know Jesus. Some are located in countries closed to the gospel, and neither their names nor their primary purpose for being there can be shared openly. These missionaries rely on monetary support from local churches and local Christ-followers like you to do their work.

Also, several organizations such as World Vision and Compassion International offer opportunities for you to sponsor underprivileged children around the world by giving them a few dollars a month, and praying for them. Other organizations such as The Voice of the Martyrs and International Christian Concern distribute periodic publications that inform the Western world about persecuted Christ-followers throughout the globe, and even provide stories, prayer requests, and ways to contact persecuted Christ-followers in their native language. The Gideons International provides copies of the Bible to soldiers, hotel rooms, and language groups in most countries around the world. All of these organizations are great opportunities through which you can help fund God's work both at home and across the globe.

But God does not simply want your money. He wants your total life. Missionaries strongly request prayer for a wide variety of situations and circumstances[2], and prayer is something any Christ-follower can provide. There are also a variety of ways to physically get involved, and get your hands dirty for God's Kingdom. For example, the national Free Will Baptist denomination offers service opportunities at its annual summer convention through events such as Impact, a one-day evangelism and service campaign, and Reach That Guy—a program for youth, which performs service projects for the underprivileged and non-Christ-followers. In addition, you can join Free Will Baptists in extending a global reach with humanitarian aid through the non-governmental organization The Hanna Project. Additionally, short-term mission trips via E-TEAM and the Truth and Peace Student Leadership Conference allow teenagers to grow their personal walk with God in ways never before thought possible. Contact information for all of the above ministries is listed in Appendix F.

Many local churches also send teams on short-term mission trips for a week or more to serve God with their hands and hearts. God leads some Christ-followers to abandon all they know to become full-time missionaries to another culture. Jesus once asked His disciples to pray for God to send people to reach others with the message of the gospel because there were so many who needed to hear it (Matthew 9:35-38). Today, the need for workers to go and build churches is still great all across the globe, particularly within the world's cities. One area in which Christ-followers have been historically weak in planting churches is the inner cities of the U.S.—cities like New York, Chicago, Los Angeles, and San Francisco. These locations and others like them continue to lack a Christian presence, but few have answered the call to go. Jesus calls His followers to share His message with those who remain lost, and these individuals inhabit the U.S. and world cities in vast numbers.

God possesses no missionary age requirement or limit. Free Will Baptist missionaries have gone to mission fields around the globe near the age of retirement, and others have left behind their professional careers or well-established ministries to begin new church plants. God does not call everyone to this endeavor, but are you ready to support missions, financially and prayerfully now, or physically if He calls you in the future?

These things will require making cuts in your budget or rearranging your schedule. Sometimes a radical life change in vocation or residence may be the result. This is what God expected of Israel in Haggai, and He still expects it today. You must give careful thought to your ways and find out what you can do to advance God's Kingdom. Being faithful will not simply manifest itself in your relationship to God; it will be put on display in how you love, serve, and support others, and especially in how you contribute through your local church to its missionaries.

List some ways the church (you and other Christ followers) can show Christ's love and share the gospel or path to follow with people who may be lost.

_____

_____

What are some organizations you can support by volunteering your time, praying for them, and by financially giving to them?

_____

_____

End Notes

[1]Hebrews 6:4-5 gives a detailed description of these people, which can only apply to Christ-followers
[2]Speak to your teacher or Bible study leader if you are interested in receiving periodically published newsletters from the missionaries your church supports. This will enable you to engage in more strategic prayer for them.

chapter 12

Your Heritage

Melvin Worthington

When hiking, you must know your position at all times. Orienteering teaches you how to travel between two known points such as a tower, which is your starting point, and a hilltop, which is your destination.

In this chapter, we will focus on the known point of where Free Will Baptists have been—or our history. Reflecting on one's heritage can be a very rich and rewarding experience.

Paul reminds Timothy to continually observe the things he learned as a child, remembering those who taught him (2 Timothy 3:13-15). Paul further challenged the Christ-followers in Thessalonica to stand fast and hold to the traditions they had been taught (2 Thessalonians 2:15).

Helping each generation of Free Will Baptists understand your heritage will help you appreciate denominational doctrine and distinctives. Every generation must ask and answer the questions: Who are we? What do we believe? What are our distinctives? How do we operate?

Resources for reviewing and reflecting on the history and heritage of Free Will Baptists include *A Free Will Baptist Handbook: Heritage, Beliefs, and Ministries* by Dr. J. Matthew Pinson and *The Free Will Baptists in America 1727—1984* by William F. Davidson. These two works provide a concise perspective on the history and heritage of Free Will Baptists. *The Treatise of the Faith and Practices of the National Association of Free Will Baptists, Inc.* is an excellent resource as well. The Executive Office of the National Association of Free Will Baptists, Inc. (NAFWB) publishes this work. Included in the *Treatise* is the Church Covenant, The Faith of Free Will Baptists, The Articles of Faith, The Practices of Free Will Baptists, and The Constitution of the NAFWB.

AN OVERVIEW OF CHURCH HISTORY

The best resource for church history is the Bible. The book of Acts is a divine, dependable, and descriptive record of the history of the early church. Reading through the book, you can see God establishing the beginnings of what would be the place where families met together to fulfill the Great Commission. The Great Commission is reaching, teaching, and causing this cycle to repeat (Matthew 28:18-20).

Jesus declared He would build His church (Matthew 16:13-20). The word *church* is used in three ways in the New Testament. The first way it is used is to describe the *Lord's church*. It is the universal church, the members of the body of Christ or all Christ's followers. A second way the word is used in the New Testament is to describe a *local church*. The local church is an organized body of Christ-followers who assemble to worship God according to Scripture. The local church is located within a single geographical location The third way the word is used in the New Testament is to describe the *larger church*. Acts 13, 15, and 1 Corinthians 1 are examples of this usage. It refers to a group of churches which come together to render decisions as a group. The district associations in the Free Will Baptist denomination are composed of local churches. For example, when the government addresses the denomination, it often refers to the whole denomination as the *Free Will Baptist church* as in the third definition. Other examples include the Wesleyan Church, the Nazarene church, and the Presbyterian church. In Acts 15, when the church held a council to address specific issues, more than one local church met. This implies the word *church* is used to designate more than one local church.

The book of Acts records the word being used in all three ways. It is important to determine how the word is used when studying the book of Acts. Acts is a historical record of the early church (Acts 1:1). Perhaps the best way to have a biblical view of church history is to read the book of Acts, which is the inspired record of the story of the church.

Acts 1 records the ascension of Jesus into the heavens. Following His ascension, the angels appeared and announced that He would return in the same manner. Acts 2 records the advent of the Comforter. The Holy Spirit descended and took up His residence in all those who believed in Jesus. This was the fulfillment of Jesus' promise in Luke 24:49 and Acts 1:8. Acts 3—28 records the advancement of the church. Beginning with 120 Christ-followers (Acts 1:15) in the upper room, the church grew to 3,000, and then to 5,000. Acts 2:41-47; 4:32-37 provides a description of practices, which characterized the early church. By Acts 9:31, local churches had been established in Judea, Galilee, and Samaria. As a result of the Holy Spirit's power working amidst Paul and the other apostles' ministries, the church grew from Jerusalem throughout Asia and North Africa into Europe.

As the church spread, it faced varying degrees of persecution, popularity, and purity. During the Middle Ages, the Roman Catholic church became a dominate political power, but did not maintain a pure doctrine of biblical Christianity. The faithful church was often persecuted as heretics by the political and religious organizations. But those who held to the apostles' doctrine continued to persevere in churches separate from Catholicism.

In 1517, a major event took place that changed the course of church history—the Protestant Reformation. It was also known as the Protestant Revolt. It was a Christian reform movement led by Martin Luther, John Calvin, and other early Protestants. This movement established Protestantism as a constituent branch of contemporary Christianity. At the heart of this reformation was a commitment to the biblical truth of *salvation by faith alone*. For Martin Luther, "the freedom of the will" was a key issue. The doctrines of the papacy, purgatory, or indulgences were not the key issues for Luther; in his mind, the real issue was the doctrine of the freedom of the will. Those who championed the Protestant Reformation protested the doctrines, rituals, and ecclesiastical structure of the Roman Catholic church. This led to the creation of Protestant churches.

What two books could you read to learn more about the history of Free Will Baptists?

_____

_____

What book in the Bible do you read to learn about the early history of the church?

_____

AN OVERVIEW OF FREE WILL BAPTIST HISTORY

Free Will Baptists are not a new group. They have been in existence since the 16th century. Free Will Baptists share a doctrine that can be traced to the apostles, not in physical records, but in common beliefs. Matthew Pinson's book, *A Free Will Baptist Handbook: Heritage, Beliefs, and Ministries* gives an excellent summary of why Free Will Baptists came to be called *Free Will*. The concepts of free will, free grace, and free salvation have been the hallmarks of Free Will Baptists since the formation of the group. It is interesting that the doctrine of the freedom of the will was also a key issue in the Protestant Reformation. Although the rise of Free Will Baptist can be traced to the influence of Baptists of Arminian persuasion who settled in the North American colonies from England, it is important to emphasize that the National Association of Free Will Baptists, Inc. was organized as a denomination in 1935. In light of this, the current overview will primarily address Free Will Baptist history leading up to that date.

The Men

The denomination sprang up on two fronts at almost the same time.

The southern line, or Palmer movement, traces its beginnings to the year 1727 when one Paul Palmer organized a church at Chowan, North Carolina. Palmer had previously ministered in New Jersey and Maryland, having been baptized in a congregation that had moved from Wales to a tract on the Delaware River in northern Pennsylvania.[1]

The northern line, or Randall movement, had its beginnings with a congregation organized by Benjamin Randall on June 30, 1780, in New Durham, New Hampshire. Both lines of Free Will Baptists taught the doctrine of free grace, free salvation, and free will, although from the first there was no organizational connection between them.[2]

The Merger

The northern line expanded more rapidly in the beginning and extended its outreach into the west and southwest. In 1910-1911, this body of Free Will Baptists merged with the Northern Baptist denomination, taking more than half its 1,100 churches and all denominational property, including several major colleges. On December 28, 1916, at Pattonsburg, Missouri, representatives of the remnant churches in the Randall movement reorganized into the Cooperative General Association of Free Will Baptists.[3]

Free Will Baptists in the southeastern United States, having descended from the Palmer foundation, had often manifested fraternal relationships with Free Will Baptists of the Randall movement in the north and west, but the slavery question and the Civil War prevented formal union between them. The churches in the southern line were organized into various associations and conferences from the beginning, and had finally organized into a General Conference by

1921. These congregations were not affected by the merger of the northern movement with the Northern Baptists.[4]

The Movement

After the remnants of the Randall movement reorganized into the Cooperative General Association and the Palmer movement organized into the General Conference, it was inevitable that a fusion of the two groups of Free Will Baptists would finally occur. In Nashville, Tennessee, on November 5, 1935, representatives of these two groups met and organized the National Association of Free Will Baptists. This body adopted a common treatise, which set forth the basic doctrines and described the faith and practice that had characterized Free Will Baptists through the years. Having been revised on several occasions, it serves as a guideline for a denominational fellowship, which comprises more than 2,400 churches in North America and more than 1,000 churches around the world in other countries beyond North America.[5]

The national offices are located in the metropolitan area of Nashville, Tennessee. Agencies operating within the national offices include the Executive Office, International Missions, Home Missions, Retirement and Insurance, the Free Will Baptist Foundation, Master's Men, and Women Nationally Active for Christ. Free Will Baptist Bible College is located in the same metro area on its own separate campus. Randall House, the Free Will Baptist publishing group, is also located in Nashville, Tennessee within its own separate facility.

The Mission

The Free Will Baptist denomination is a fellowship of evangelical Christ-followers united in extending the witness of Jesus and the building of His Church throughout the world.[6]

The Organizational Structure of the National Association of Free Will Baptists, Inc.

Free Will Baptist Churches, while independent and autonomous, do not practice isolation. They form associations with one another in several levels of organization. It is to be remembered, however, that these associations are voluntary, both at their beginning and in their continuation. The local church retains at all times the liberty to withdraw from the association it has voluntarily joined.[7]

From reading the first section, how far back can historians document the existence of Free Will Baptists? _____

Where did the two earliest fronts (works) begin in Free Will Baptists and who was the leader for each?

_____

_____

The merger in 1910-1911 caused a loss as a significant number left Free Will Baptist and merged with the Northern Baptist. What was lost in the merger?

_____

_____

What date did the current Free Will Baptist reorganize and where did this occur?

_____

_____

Re-write the mission of Free Will Baptist in your own words.

_____

_____

_____

_____

The Observation

Free Will Baptists are not interdenominational, independents, or non-denominational but possess a distinct organizational structure. Distinct doctrines and practices are evident from the history and heritage. For more information about these distinctives, doctrines, and practices, read through the small booklet entitled *Treatise of Faith and Practices of the National Association of Free Will Baptists, Inc.* Forgetting these truths will prevent members from perpetuating the denominational distinctives.

The Organization

The organizational structure of the NAFWB is in an ever-widening circle. From the individual member, to the local church, to the district association, to the state association, to the national association, the circles continue to grow wider. Within every wider circle there are relationships and responsibilities. This pattern of organization is implied in Acts 1:8. The first circle is that of the individual Christ follower—the ambassador. All the other circles in the organizational structure are dependent upon the ambassador. God declares you are His ambassador (2 Corinthians 5:18-21). The next broader circle is that of the local church—the assembly. Christ-followers voluntarily join together to form a local church. The Free Will Baptist Church Covenant states precepts and practices for members of the local church. The next broader circle includes the district, state, and national relationships—the associations.

The objectives of the denomination include evangelism, education, edification, enlistment, and encouragement. The outcome is that a Christ-follower rightly related to a local church that is rightly related to the district association that is rightly related to a state association that is rightly related to the national association is afforded the opportunity to engage in a world-wide ministry.

The Agencies

The agencies of the NAFWB may be divided into four groups: the executive office, the standing boards and their respective departments, the women's ministry, and the commissions.

The Executive Office

The Executive Office serves as the administrative office of the denomination. Its purpose is to serve the national body, various boards, state organizations, local churches, and individual members of the denomination. The office is staffed by an executive secretary whose responsibility includes administration, general promotion, public relations, publications, stewardship, arranging the annual convention, and managing the national offices.

The Standing Boards & Departments

The standing boards include The Board of Trustees of Free Will Baptist Bible College, The Board of International Missions, The Board of Home Missions, The Board of Retirement and Insurance, The Masters Men Board, The Board of Sunday School and Church Training, and The Board of Trustees of the Free Will Baptist Foundation.

All of the boards are comprised of nine men with the exception of The Board of Trustees of the Free Will Baptist Foundation, which possesses 18 members. Each of these boards plans a program and supervises the operations within its respective field, and is responsible for all its actions to the NAFWB. Each board also operates under its own constitution and by-laws, which must be approved by the NAFWB. At the beginning of each fiscal year, each board submits a budget both to the NAFWB for approval and an independent public accountant for external auditing.

The *International Missions Department* exists to facilitate church planting movements among unreached peoples. A church planting movement is the exponential multiplication of local church plants within a given people group or population segment. Church growth and multiplication may take place after a series of human actions and events; however, ultimately any truly spiritual movement depends more on the Holy Spirit of God than people.

The *Home Missions Department* exists to exalt Jesus Christ and fulfill the Great Commission by using the efforts of missionaries and chaplains to communicate the Gospel, make disciples, and plant new churches in the United States, Canada, Mexico, and the U.S. territories, such as the Virgin Islands and Puerto Rico.

Welch College exists to educate leaders to serve Christ, His Church, and His world through Biblical thought and life.

The *Free Will Baptist Foundation* exists as the planned giving arm of the Free Will Baptist denomination whose purpose is to connect Free Will Baptist donors with all ministries of the denomination through planned giving, endowments, and money management.

The *Free Will Baptist Board of Retirement* is committed to serve the Lord and His church by helping our pastors, missionaries, and lay employees achieve financial security in retirement. We accomplish this by providing a high-quality retirement savings plan designed to help them reach their retirement goals and enable them to live their retirement years in dignity.

Randall House exists to promote the cause of Christ and serve the church through the development and distribution of excellent, economical, effective, and evangelistic Bible-based curriculum, products, training, and events. Randall House works to build believers through church and home.

The *Master's Men Department* exists to enlist laymen and pastors in their local churches to encourage stewardship and fellowship and to deepen their spiritual lives in accordance with the tenets and doctrines of the Free Will Baptists.

The Women's Ministry

The *Women Nationally Active for Christ (WNAC)* is recognized as subordinate to the National Association; but it can organize at its own discretion and have power to create and adopt a constitution and by-laws and maintain complete management of the work for which it is constituted. WNAC is an auxiliary arm of the National Association of Free Will Baptists. It exists to help each woman fulfill the Great Commission through her God-designed roles in the home, church, community, and world. Recognizing and respecting pastoral leadership, WNAC desires to assist local congregations in implementing and encouraging thriving Bible-based, outwardly focused women's groups and networking them together in order to accomplish greater Kingdom goals.

The Commissions

The NAFWB also maintains the following commissions: the Commission for Theological Integrity, the Historical Commission, the Media Commission, and the Music Commission.

AN OVERVIEW OF THE INTERNATIONAL FELLOWSHIP OF FREE WILL BAPTIST CHURCHES

The Dream

The International Fellowship of Free Baptist Churches was born out of a desire on the part of missionaries to have an organization that would promote fellowship among the various countries where Free Will Baptist work existed. In light of this expressed desire, the Executive Office and the International Missions Department cooperated to study the feasibility of such an organization. Various other denominations including the Assemblies of God, Christian Missionary Alliance, the Church of the Nazarene, and the Wesleyan Church were consulted regarding their international work in order to explore the possibilities for Free Will Baptists.

The Development

Representatives from Japan, Canada, Mexico, Brazil, Panama, Uruguay, and the United States met on August 24-27, 1992 in Panama and voted to organize the International Fellowship of Free Will Baptists Churches. The representative group adopted the Panama Declaration of 1992, affirming their commitment to the fundamental beliefs of orthodox Christianity, those distinctive beliefs and practices that uniquely characterize Free Will Baptists, the necessity of holy living, the dangers of the ecumenical movement, and the priority of evangelism. The International Fellowship of Free Will Baptist Churches that began in 1995 meets every three years for the purpose of "identification, communion, and mutual edification and encouragement in order to better fulfill the Great Commission of evangelism and the establishing of churches among all peoples." (Citation charter of the International Fellowship of Free Will Baptist Churches, Inc.) The nature and organizational structure of the International Fellowship of Free Will Baptist Churches was to be a "fraternal fellowship of autonomous national bodies" without ecclesiastical hierarchy or legislative power over the member associations.

The National Association of Free Will Baptists possesses a rich history and heritage. The organizational structure, objectives stated, and the opportunities shared provide the individual Christ-follower the opportunity to reach the entire world with the Gospel.

It is important that you find your place in the Free Will Baptist family. You are a necessary part of the carrying forward of a legacy. The reality is that Free Will Baptists are distinct, and yet diverse. This dichotomy is not a weakness, but rather a strength. Free Will Baptists should be proud, in a good sense, of their history and heritage.

Your Church's Story

This would be a good time to discuss the history and story of how your local church was formed, and what larger ministries it supports. Ask about your district and state associations and about the available opportunities for interacting with the national association. Consider traveling to the annual national convention with your family, and experience the larger Free Will Baptist body worshiping with all ages in their respective services, seminars, and activities.

How did your church begin and what purpose does it serve in your community?

_____

_____

Based on what your church is currently doing how would your community describe the impact it has on the families in the community?

_____

_____

End Notes

[1] *Treatise of the Faith and Practices of the National Association of Free Will Baptists, Inc.*, Preface
[2] Et al.
[3] Et al.
[4] Et al.
[5] Et al.
[6] Et al.
[7] *Treatise of the Faith and Practices of the National Association of Free Will Baptists, Inc.*, 47.

appendix A
How We Received the Bible

It is important to recognize how we received the Bible and just how it was put together. In doing so, we must understand that the Bible is God's inspired words and in it, we discover our spiritual condition, God's plan of salvation through Christ, and strength and wisdom to live the best kind of life. The Bible wasn't all written at the same time, but each book within the Bible was penned over a span of 1,500 years by as many as 40 different people. These writers were not considered "best sellers" of their day; there was no power or prestige for them, but each suffered adversity, persecution, and some even death for believing and writing the message of the Gospel.

Wouldn't the original become more and more tainted after generations of being copied?

In questioning the transmission or translation of the Bible, we are talking about how the contents of the Bible were passed down through history. After all, if that was done poorly, then what we are viewing as the inspired word of God is questionable, but if we have reliable copies of the original that were passed down with great care, we can trust its writings.

The truth is that the entire Bible has been passed down from generation to generation with astounding accuracy. Through the centuries, the original Old Testament writings were preserved with incredible care. Scribes carefully copied letter by letter, word for word, line by line. They knew they were preserving and distributing the very Word of God. They took their jobs so seriously they would record the number of times letters occurred in the books, the number of words and verses, and the middle words and verses of passages. This helps us have an even greater understanding of Jesus' words in Matthew 5:18 when He explains that not even one jot or tittle would pass from the Law without being fulfilled—not the smallest letter or even part of a letter.

Jesus knew the Scriptures very well. He quoted from every section of the Hebrew Scriptures: Law, Prophets, and Writings. Jesus put His stamp of authenticity and authority on the Old Testament. The Dead Sea Scrolls, discovered in 1949, confirmed that the Old Testament we have today was the same as in the days of Jesus.

We have over 5,600 manuscript copies of various portions of the New Testament. Not only that, but there are many different translations in various languages from as early as the fourth century, which illustrate that the message of the Gospel has remained the same. There is remarkable agreement in the manuscript copies, helping us to see that the Word of God remains unchanged even to this day. You can trust the Bible that you hold, taking into account the great price the original writers paid to pen each book, how it was treated with extreme reverence and honor down through the centuries of copying and translating, and how it ultimately came to you.

What do you mean when you say that the Bible is "inspired?"

How is the Bible not just a human invention and opinions of men? When we say the Bible is inspired by God, we mean that it is God-breathed. 2 Timothy 3:16 tells us that every single bit of Scripture is God-breathed; therefore, the Bible is a library of books that was written by Spirit-moved authors recording God-breathed words, sentences, and concepts. These human writers were moved by God to accurately pen what God wanted them to preserve for all humanity. He didn't put them into a trance, or dictate what was to be written, but the Holy Spirit guided them to write what He wanted written and preserved them from error in the process. Each book was written by real people, recording real historical events, and communicating God's real, inspired truth.

But how was the Bible actually put together?

The books of the Old Testament were written by various prophets of God and Jewish scribes and historians. The same process of inspiration was involved in the New Testament Scripture. Most of it was written by the apostles of Jesus (Matthew, John, Peter, Paul) and those who worked closely with the apostles (Mark and Luke). All of the New Testament was written during the time the apostles lived and, in effect, had apostolic authority. The early Christians collected their writings and shared them among the churches. By the second and third century, early church writers were recording lists of the various books that were being used by the Christian church.

In later centuries, other letters were written but not were not recognized as Scripture. These other books were not accepted largely because they failed in at least one of the following questions:

1. Apostolic authority–was it written by an apostle or one closely associated with the apostles?

2. Orthodoxy–was it in harmony with apostolic doctrine and basic teachings of Christianity?

3. Church approved–was it received and recognized by the whole church from the earliest days?

We should avoid the mistaken notion that men decided what would be the Word of God or that men decided truth. The church councils of the Middle Ages did not decide what would be in the Bible or what would be correct doctrine. More accurately, the church councils merely declared to what degree they understood and accepted what the Bible taught. They got some things right, they got some things wrong. Sometimes later councils disagreed with earlier councils. These councils had no authority to confirm or establish any Bible doctrine. They did not have the apostolic authority of the Jerusalem Council in Acts 15.

In spite of numerous attempts by carnal men through the centuries to suppress or distort the word of God, God has been faithful to ensure that His "instruction book" for life is still available for us today. You can be confident that the Bible you hold in your hand or read from your electronic device is the very Word of God.

appendix B

Study Tools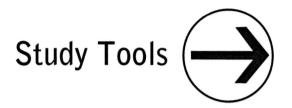

To best study the Bible, you need to choose the right tools to aid you in your learning. Most of these tools are available for free online; however if you want to obtain a few for your personal library, here are some suggestions:

Bible Dictionary: There are many trustworthy Bible dictionaries out there, among them are the *Anchor Bible Dictionary*, a 6-volume set, making it one of the most complete dictionaries out there, and then the *Evangelical Dictionary*, which is an in-depth explanation of biblical terms and even doctrinal and philosophical positions. *Holmans, Vines, Strong's,* and *Naves* are all great for shorter definitions of biblical terms.

Commentaries: There are several wonderful volumes of commentaries out there these days to help you best understand Scripture. Among them are the volumes of *R. Kent Hughes* (he includes a systematic approach toward the text in an easy to comprehend style of writing while also including illustrations and practical application for each passage), *The Randall House Commentary* series (which offers verse-by-verse study method, summaries and application notes), and *The Bible Exposition Commentary* by Warren Wiersbe (which brings extensive Bible knowledge through various Old and New Testament volumes).

Concordance: Probably the best and most used concordance out there is the *Strong's Concordance.* It is pretty easy to use and understand while also being a thorough and complete tool in understanding Scripture.

Lexicon: Probably one of the newer and best lexicons is *The Hebrew and Aramaic Lexicon of the Old and New Testaments*, which is a multi-volume set that breaks down every verse in Scripture, providing the original language, word definitions, and an exhaustive list of other places in the Bible that word or phrase occurs. It is also available on CD if you would prefer a digital copy.

FREE RESOURCES:

Two of the best websites out there to use as study tools are:

-**www.blueletterbible.org:** This website combines various concordances, Greek and Hebrew lexicons, audio commentaries, various versions and translations of Scripture, dictionary aids, and even hymns that relate to particular verses or passages.

-**www.bibleclassics.com:** This website combines the commentaries and writings of John Calvin, John Darby, the Geneva Study Bible, John Gill, Jamieson, Faussett, and Brown, Matthew Henry (full and concise commentaries), and John Wesley. You can go to the book, passage, or verse and can see each of the above's thoughts on the Scripture. Again, this is free online and helps any passage become more clear.

OTHER ONLINE RESOURCES:

www.e-sword.net, www.biblegateway.com, and www.net.bible.org.

appendix C

How to Use Our Road Map

STUDYING DANIEL 1:1–8

Discovering the Literary and Cultural Context

According to Daniel 1, we can see that Daniel wrote this book somewhere around 537 B.C., some years after the third year of the reign of Nebuchadnezzar. During his boyhood days, Daniel would have experienced some very deep influences in his life. In the providence of God, He allowed Daniel to be born into the reign of good king, Josiah – the only good king in southern Judah.

According to a Ryrie Study Bible, Josiah was the first good king those people had had in 57 years! Before Josiah, there was a wicked king, named King Manasseh who reigned for 55 years. And after his 55 year reign, his son, Amon, came to the throne. He only lasted 2 years! He was so bad that the Scriptures say that the servants of his own house conspired against him and, when he least expected it, killed him. He was followed on the throne by Josiah, the good king, when he was only 8 years old, reigning until he was 39 with an incredibly godly time on the throne.

Cross-referencing 2 Chronicles tells us that in the eighth year of his reign, Josiah began to seek after God and in the twelve year, he began to purge Judah & Jerusalem of all the idols that were worshiped there. And so it began in the days of Josiah that the most remarkable revival that the world had ever known at that time began to take place.

Josiah was convicted about the terrible condition of the temple and so he put together a group of men who were going to go to the temple of Solomon and rebuild it. The Bible says that, while they were rebuilding the temple, they happened upon a book. And that book, was the book of the Law. The book of the Law was lost in the church.

So, cross-referencing to 2 Kings 23:2-3, we see that as they were rebuilding the temple, they found the book of the Law and the Bible says that Hilkia the priest brought the book of the Law to Shafen the scribe & Shafen the scribe came to Josiah the king and he said, "King, I want you to read this book."

And so throughout all of Josiah's reign, there was a great revival and Judah had never seen anything like, and putting the timeline together, little Daniel was running around in the kingdom during this wonderful time as a young prince in the court. This would have put Daniel right in the middle of the intimate workings of that revival.

Discovering What the Passage Says—Observation

Verse 8 seems to be the power-punch of the passage as Daniel said, "I can't do that. Scripture says that's wrong and so I have to draw a line. I can't do what the Bible forbids me to do." And that's where we're going to pick up the story of this man's uncompromising life! He refuses to compromise his life; he would not violate the Word of God. And, in skimming the rest of the book, every word, every thought of holiness falls down at the feet of verse 8 that explains that Daniel purposed in his heart to do what was right. Much of his strength and boldness must have come from what we discovered in the context—the spiritually strong environment he grew up in and the great king he served under. This short passage explains through and through that God prepared Daniel for a moment of boldness and that moment would begin a legacy of faithfulness.

Understanding What the Point of the Passage Is

Based on this passage, God's preparation of a person is a thing of wonder. When we watch it from afar, we can't help but stand back in amazement! God is always more concerned about the worker than He is the work. While we focus on the ministry, God is always focused on the minister. So when we view the man Daniel, we are tempted as always to just see what he did and how his influence was far-reaching. But what's even more dramatic is how God prepared him to be the champion he would eventually become. God was actually beginning His work in the life of Daniel long before most of the stories in the book of Daniel were written - long before 14-year old Daniel came to the palace of Babylon to be in the king's court. The point of the passage is clearly the power in God's preparation of a man.

Why Does This Matter – How to Apply This Passage

It seems that, if we were to write the story of our lives down, there would be times and places when we have made decisions that will affect all of our lives. But we also have to realize from this passage that the common experience for men and women across our country is to go to church every week and the book of the Law, for all practical purposes, might as well be lost as it was just before Daniel's day. We never open it nor obey it.

We must set out to write the words of God on our hearts so that we might know Him even more and obey His commandments. The resolution of our lives should be the same of Daniel: no matter what job we have, who we are to others, and what's going on in our lives, we must purpose in our hearts to do the right thing according to God's Word. Success is not dependent on us compromising what we're committed to. The story of compromise before Josiah's reign was not a happy one; it was a sad and devastating story. Everywhere you see compromise, you will also see loss, not gain. We should be hungry to stand up and say, just as Daniel did in this passage, "I have determined in my heart to not do wrong, but to obey God."

Scripture Memory: Daniel 1:8.

appendix D

FWB CHURCH COVENANT

Having given ourselves to God, by faith in Christ, and adopted the Word of God as our rule of faith and practice, we now give ourselves to one another by the will of God in this solemn covenant.

We promise, by His grace, to love and obey Him in all things, to avoid all appearance of evil, to abstain from all sinful amusements and unholy conformity to the world, from all sanction of the use and sale of intoxicating beverages, and to "provide things honest in the sight of all men."

We agree faithfully to discharge our obligations in reference to the study of the Scriptures, secret prayer, family devotions, and social worship; and by self-denial, faith, and good works endeavor to "grow in grace and the knowledge of our Lord and Saviour Jesus Christ."

We will not forsake the assembling of ourselves together for church conferences, public worship, and the observance of the ordinances of the Gospel; nor fail to pay according to our ability for the support of the church, of its poor, and all its benevolent work.

We agree to accept Christian admonition and reproof with meekness, and to watch over one another in love, endeavoring to "keep the unity of the Spirit" in the bonds of peace, to be careful of one another's happiness and reputation, and seek to strengthen the weak, encourage the afflicted, admonish the erring, and as far as we are able, promote the success of the church and of the Gospel.

We will everywhere hold Christian principle sacred and Christian obligations and enterprises supreme; counting it our chief business in life to extend the influence of Christ in society, constantly praying and toiling that the kingdom of God may come, and His will be done on earth as it is in heaven.

To this end we agree to labor for the promotion of educational and denominational enterprises, the support of missions, the success of Sunday schools, and evangelistic efforts for the salvation of the world. And may the God of peace sanctify us wholly, and preserve us blameless unto the coming of our Lord Jesus Christ.

appendix E
Daily Bible Reading Plan

1. Genesis 1-3
2. Genesis 4-7
3. Genesis 8-11
4. Job 1-5
5. Job 6-9
6. Job 10-13
7. Job 14-16
8. Job 17-20
9. Job 21-23
10. Job 24-28
11. Job 29-31
12. Job 32-34
13. Job 35-37
14. Job 38-39
15. Job 40-42
16. Genesis 12-15
17. Genesis 16-18
18. Genesis 19-21
19. Genesis 22-24
20. Genesis 25-26
21. Genesis 27-29
22. Genesis 30-31
23. Genesis 32-34
24. Genesis 35-37
25. Genesis 38-40
26. Genesis 41-42
27. Genesis 43-45
28. Genesis 46-47
29. Genesis 48-50
30. Exodus 1-3
31. Exodus 4-6
32. Exodus 7-9
33. Exodus 10-12
34. Exodus 13-15
35. Exodus 16-18
36. Exodus 19-21
37. Exodus 22-24
38. Exodus 25-27
39. Exodus 28-29
40. Exodus 30-32
41. Exodus 33-35
42. Exodus 36-38
43. Exodus 39-40
44. Leviticus 1-4
45. Leviticus 5-7
46. Leviticus 8-10
47. Leviticus 11-13
48. Leviticus 14-15
49. Leviticus 16-18
50. Leviticus 19-21
51. Leviticus 22-23
52. Leviticus 24-25
53. Leviticus 26-27
54. Numbers 1-2
55. Numbers 3-4
56. Numbers 5-6
57. Numbers 7
58. Numbers 8-10
59. Numbers 11-13
60. Numbers 14-15; Psalm 90

61. Numbers 16-17
62. Numbers 18-20
63. Numbers 21-22
64. Numbers 23-25
65. Numbers 26-27
66. Numbers 28-30
67. Numbers 31-32
68. Numbers 33-34
69. Numbers 35-36
70. Deuteronomy 1-2
71. Deuteronomy 3-4
72. Deuteronomy 5-7
73. Deuteronomy 8-10
74. Deuteronomy 11-13
75. Deuteronomy 14-16
76. Deuteronomy 17-20
77. Deuteronomy 21-23
78. Deuteronomy 24-27
79. Deuteronomy 28-29
80. Deuteronomy 30-31
81. Deuteronomy 32-34; Psalm 91
82. Joshua 1-4
83. Joshua 5-8
84. Joshua 9-11
85. Joshua 12-15
86. Joshua 16-18
87. Joshua 19-21
88. Joshua 22-24
89. Judges 1-2
90. Judges 3-5
91. Judges 6-7
92. Judges 8-9
93. Judges 10-12
94. Judges 13-15
95. Judges 16-18
96. Judges 19-21
97. Ruth
98. 1 Samuel 1-3
99. 1 Samuel 4-8
100. 1 Samuel 9-12
101. 1 Samuel 13-14
102. 1 Samuel 15-17
103. 1 Samuel 18-20; Psalms 11, 59
104. 1 Samuel 21-24
105. Psalms 7, 27, 31, 34, 52
106. Psalms 56, 120, 140-142
107. 1 Samuel 25-27
108. Psalms 17, 35, 54, 63
109. 1 Samuel 28-31; Psalms 18
110. Psalms 121, 123-125, 128-130
111. 2 Samuel 1-4
112. Psalms 6, 8-10, 14, 16, 19, 21
113. 1 Chronicles 1-2
114. Psalms 43-45, 49, 84-85, 87
115. 1 Chronicles 3-5
116. Psalms 73, 77-78
117. 1 Chronicles 6
118. Psalms 81, 88, 92-93
119. 1 Chronicles 7-10
120. Psalms 102-104

121. 2 Samuel 5; 1 Chronicles 11-12
122. Psalms 133
123. Psalms 106-107
124. 1 Chronicles 13-16
125. Psalms 1-2, 15, 22-24, 47, 68
126. Psalms 89, 96, 100-101, 105, 132
127. 2 Samuel 6-7; 1 Chronicles 17
128. Psalms 25, 29, 33, 36, 39
129. 2 Samuel 8-9; 1 Chronicles 18
130. Psalms 50, 53, 60, 75
131. 2 Samuel 10; 1 Chronicles 19;
     Psalms 20
132. Psalms 65-67, 69-70
133. 2 Samuel 11-12; 1 Chronicles 20
134. Psalms 32, 51, 86, 122
135. 2 Samuel 13-15
136. Psalms 3-4, 12-13, 28, 55
137. 2 Samuel 16-18
138. Psalms 26, 40, 58, 61-62, 64
139. 2 Samuel 19-21
140. Psalms 5, 38, 41-42
141. 2 Samuel 22-23; Psalms 57
142. Psalms 95, 97-99
143. 2 Samuel 24; 1 Chronicles 21-22;
     Psalms 30
144. Psalms 108-110
145. 1 Chronicles 23-25
146. Psalms 131, 138-139, 143-145
147. 1 Chronicles 26-29; Psalms 127
148. Psalms 111-118
149. 1 Kings 1-2; Psalms 37, 71, 94
150. Psalm 119
151. 1 Kings 3-4
152. 2 Chronicles 1; Psalms 72
153. Song of Solomon
154. Proverbs 1-3
155. Proverbs 4-6
156. Proverbs 7-9
157. Proverbs 10-12
158. Proverbs 13-15
159. Proverbs 16-18
160. Proverbs 19-21
161. Proverbs 22-24
162. 1 Kings 5-6; 2 Chronicles 2-3
163. 1 Kings 7; 2 Chronicles 4
164. 1 Kings 8; 2 Chronicles 5
165. 2 Chronicles 6-7; Psalms 136
166. Psalms 134, 146-150
167. 1 Kings 9; 2 Chronicles 8
168. Proverbs 25-26
169. Proverbs 27-29
170. Ecclesiastes 1-6
171. Ecclesiastes 7-12
172. 1 Kings 10-11; 2 Chronicles 9
173. Proverbs 30-31
174. 1 Kings 12-14
175. 2 Chronicles 10-12
176. 1 Kings 15; 2 Chronicles 13-16
177. 1 Kings 16; 2 Chronicles 17
178. 1 Kings 17-19

179. 1 Kings 20-21
180. 1 Kings 22; 2 Chronicles 18
181. 2 Chronicles 19-23
182. Obadiah; Psalms 82-83
183. 2 Kings 1-4
184. 2 Kings 5-8
185. 2 Kings 9-11
186. 2 Kings 12-13; 2 Chronicles 24
187. 2 Kings 14; 2 Chronicles 25
188. Jonah
189. 2 Kings 15; 2 Chronicles 26
190. Isaiah 1-4
191. Isaiah 5-8
192. Amos 1-5
193. Amos 6-9
194. 2 Chronicles 27; Isaiah 9-12
195. Micah
196. 2 Chronicles 28; 2 Kings 16-17
197. Isaiah 13-17
198. Isaiah 18-22
199. Isaiah 23-27
200. 2 Kings 18;
       2 Chronicles 29-31; Psalms 48
201. Hosea 1-7
202. Hosea 8-14
203. Isaiah 28-30
204. Isaiah 31-34
205. Isaiah 35-36
206. Isaiah 37-39; Psalms 76
207. Isaiah 40-43
208. Isaiah 44-48
209. 2 Kings 19; Psalms 46, 80, 135
210. Isaiah 49-53
211. Isaiah 54-58
212. Isaiah 59-63
213. Isaiah 64-66
214. 2 Kings 20-21
215. 2 Chronicles 32-33
216. Nahum
217. 2 Kings 22-23; 2 Chronicles 34-35
218. Zephaniah
219. Jeremiah 1-3
220. Jeremiah 4-6
221. Jeremiah 7-9
222. Jeremiah 10-13
223. Jeremiah 14-17
224. Jeremiah 18-22
225. Jeremiah 23-25
226. Jeremiah 26-29
227. Jeremiah 30-31
228. Jeremiah 32-34
229. Jeremiah 35-37
230. Jeremiah 38-40; Psalms 74, 79
231. 2 Kings 24-25; 2 Chronicles 36
232. Habakkuk
233. Jeremiah 41-45
234. Jeremiah 46-48
235. Jeremiah 49-50
236. Jeremiah 51-52
237. Lamentations 1-2
238. Lamentations 3-5
239. Ezekiel 1-4
240. Ezekiel 5-8

241. Ezekiel 9-12
242. Ezekiel 13-15
243. Ezekiel 16-17
244. Ezekiel 18-20
245. Ezekiel 21-22
246. Ezekiel 23-24
247. Ezekiel 25-27
248. Ezekiel 28-30
249. Ezekiel 31-33
250. Ezekiel 34-36
251. Ezekiel 37-39
252. Ezekiel 40-42
253. Ezekiel 43-45
254. Ezekiel 46-48
255. Joel
256. Daniel 1-3
257. Daniel 4-6
258. Daniel 7-9
259. Daniel 10-12
260. Ezra 1-3
261. Ezra 4-6; Psalms 137
262. Haggai
263. Zechariah 1-4
264. Zechariah 5-9
265. Zechariah 10-14
266. Esther 1-5
267. Esther 6-10
268. Ezra 7-10
269. Nehemiah 1-5
270. Nehemiah 6-7
271. Nehemiah 8-10
272. Nehemiah 11-13; Psalms 126
273. Malachi
274. Luke 1; John 1
275. Matthew 1; Luke 2
276. Matthew 2
277. Matthew 3; Mark 1; Luke 3
278. Matthew 4; Luke 4-5
279. John 2-4
280. Matthew 8; Mark 2
281. John 5
282. Matthew 12; Mark 3; Luke 6
283. Matthew 5-7
284. Matthew 9; Luke 7
285. Matthew 11
286. Luke 11
287. Matthew 13; Luke 8
288. Mark 4-5
289. Matthew 10
290. Matthew 14; Mark 6; Luke 9
291. John 6
292. Matthew 15; Mark 7
293. Matthew 16; Mark 8
294. Matthew 17; Mark 9
295. Matthew 18
296. John 7-8
297. John 9-10
298. Luke 10
299. Luke 12-13
300. Luke 14-15
301. Luke 16-17
302. John 11
303. Luke 18

304. Matthew 19; Mark 10
305. Matthew 20-21
306. Luke 19
307. Mark 11; John 12
308. Matthew 22; Mark 12
309. Matthew 23; Luke 20-21
310. Mark 13
311. Matthew 24
312. Matthew 25
313. Matthew 26; Mark 14
314. Luke 22; John 13
315. John 14-17
316. Matthew 27; Mark 15
317. Luke 23; John 18-19
318. Matthew 28; Mark 16
319. Luke 24; John 20-21
320. Acts 1-3
321. Acts 4-6
322. Acts 7-8
323. Acts 9-10
324. Acts 11-12
325. Acts 13-14
326. James
327. Acts 15-16
328. Galatians 1-3
329. Galatians 4-6
330. Acts 17
331. 1 & 2 Thessalonians
332. Acts 18-19
333. 1 Corinthians 1-4
334. 1 Corinthians 5-8
335. 1 Corinthians 9-11
336. 1 Corinthians 12-14
337. 1 Corinthians 15-16
338. 2 Corinthians 1-4
339. 2 Corinthians 5-9
340. 2 Corinthians 10-13
341. Romans 1-3
342. Romans 4-7
343. Romans 8-10
344. Romans 11-13
345. Romans 14-16
346. Acts 20-23
347. Acts 24-26
348. Acts 27-28
349. Colossians, Philemon
350. Ephesians
351. Philippians
352. 1 Timothy
353. Titus
354. 1 Peter
355. Hebrews 1-6
356. Hebrews 7-10
357. Hebrews 11-13
358. 2 Timothy
359. 2 Peter, Jude
360. 1 John
361. 2, 3 John
362. Revelation 1-5
363. Revelation 6-11
364. Revelation 12-18
365. Revelation 19-22

appendix F

Resomeces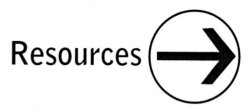

The following books would be helpful for further study:

Understanding Assurance & Salvation
by Robert E. Picirilli

The Washing of the Saints Feet
by J. Matthew Pinson

Grace, Faith, Free Will by Robert E. Picirilli

Free Will Baptist Treatise
by National Association of Free Will Baptists

Randall House Bible Commentary Series
– includes Mark, John, Romans, 1 and 2
Corinthians, Galatians-Colossians, 1 Thessalonians-Philemon, Hebrews, James, 1 and 2
Peter, Jude, 1, 2, and 3 John and Revelation.

To order products call 800-877-7030 or visit www.randallhouse.com.

Contact Information for FWB National Agencies

Board of Retirement
877.767.7738
www.boardofretirement.com

Executive Office
877.767.7659
www.nafwb.org

Free Will Baptist Foundation
877.336.7575
www.fwbgifts.org

Home Missions
877.767.7674
www.homemissions.net

International Missions
877.767.7736
www.fwbgo.com

Master's Men
877.767.8039
www.fwbmastersmen.org

ONE Magazine
877.767.7659
www.onemag.org

Randall House
800.877.7030
www.randallhouse.com

Welch College
800.763.9222
www.Welch.edu

Women Nationally Active for Christ
877.767.7662
www.wnac.org

About the Authors

General Editor

Ron Hunter Jr. has been married to his college sweetheart, Pamela, since 1987, and they have a son and a daughter named Michael and Lauren. Since 2002, Ron has served as executive director and CEO of Randall House. Ron's distinct approach to leadership, blending creative style and visionary outlook, has led Randall House into many new arenas and ministry directions including beginning the D6 Curriculum and D6 Conference. He wrote *Toy Box Leadership* published by Thomas Nelson and translated into two other languages. He has written over 30 articles for eight different magazines in addition to the Leader Profile column he writes for ONE Magazine. Ron served in ministry in both Florida and Tennessee for eleven years before his present role as CEO. He has earned his Bachelor's of Arts degree in Bible and Pastoral Training from FWBBC, Masters in Public Administration in non-profit management from the University of Colorado and is currently working on his PhD in Leadership at Dallas Baptist University.

Authors

Dale Burden married Jane Berry in 1955. He pastored for 40 years with 30 of those years at Gateway and now serves as seniors' pastor also at Gateway. Dale earned a B.A. Free Will Baptist Bible College, M.A. Columbia Bible College (now Columbia International University) Columbia, South Carolina, and has made dozens of overseas mission trips. Dale wrote the *Bible Scholar* adult Sunday school student lessons for 16 years and currently writes a new adult study for the D6 Curriculum of Sunday school called *Heritage Bible Study Series.* His passion is to see believers return to holy living and reach people for Christ.

Gowdy Cannon moved to Chicago in 2002 and served as the Youth Pastor of Northwest Community Church for over 8 years before becoming the church's pastor of bilingual ministry in 2011. His vision is for people of different languages and nations to worship together and live in daily community together. He has a degree in Bible and Theology from Free Will Baptist Bible College and pursuing a Master's degree in Intercultural Studies at Moody Theological Seminary.

Casey Cariker and wife Andrea have been married since 1998. Both Casey and Andrea graduated from Mid-America Christian University, and Casey went on to do his graduate work at Moody Bible Institute. They have also served at Rejoice Church in Owasso, OK since 1998. Casey has worked in the capacity of student ministry pastor, associate pastor, teaching pastor, and became the lead pastor in January 2011. His passion is to lead generations of our neighbors and nations to follow Jesus!

Paul Harrison, married to the former Diane Beasley since 1978, is the father of two sons (Andrew and Adam) and the grandfather of one (Charlotte Rose, "Charlie"). He has served as pastor of Cross Timbers Free Will Baptist Church in Nashville, Tennessee, since 1991. For about seventeen of those years, he served as adjunct professor at Free Will Baptist Bible College, teaching either church history or Greek. His work on the epistles of James and Jude appears in the *Randall House Bible Commentary*, and he has written various other articles for publication. He is a graduate of Free Will Baptist Bible College (B.A.), Middle Tennessee State University (M.A.), and Mid-America Baptist Theological Seminary (M.Div., Th.D.). He loves studying preachers and sermons from days gone by.

Rodney Holloman received a Bachelor of Arts in Bible and Pastoral Theology in 1992 from Southeastern Free Will Baptist College. After completing a Master of Arts in Biblical Exposition at Pensacola Christian College in 1996, he married the former Andrea Cook. God has blessed them with a daughter and son. Since college graduation, he has been a youth pastor, associate pastor, and pastor. Since 2003, Rodney has served as a professor at Southeastern and Chair of the Bible Department. He enjoys serving local churches as an interim pastor. His passions of preaching, missionary work, and personal study feed his consuming desire to help young people and young adults learn and apply God's Word to their lives and to share Him with others.

Greg McAllister married Debbie Wright in 1977, the same year he entered ministry. Greg has served as children's minister, youth pastor, discipleship director, or senior pastor in five Free Will Baptist Churches in Oklahoma, Missouri, and California. His passion is making disciples and enabling them live out their particular passions in ministry. He received his B.A. from Hillsdale FWB College (Moore, OK) in 1978 and his M.Div. from Mennonite Brethren Biblical Seminary (Fresno, CA) in 1997. Greg has previously published a book on discipleship. From 1995-2000 he served as Academic Dean at California Christian College (Fresno), and from 2003-2006 he was Senior Chaplain for the Fresno Police Department. In 2010 he was elected to the Free Will Baptist International Missions Board. In 2011, he planted a church in Clovis, California.

Robert Morgan is the pastor of The Donelson Fellowship in Nashville, Tennessee, where he has served for over 31 years. He is a best-selling and Gold-Medallion winning writer with over 25 books in print and over 3.5 million in print circulation, and is now a brand author of B & H Publishing. His products in electronic and audio format number hundreds of thousands. He is also a staff writer for Dr. David Jeremiah and *Turning Points Magazine*, and has many articles published in other leading Christian periodicals. His books have been translated into Spanish, Dutch, Russian, Chinese, Indonesian, and Korean. Rob has appeared on numerous national television and radio shows, such as *Life Today with James and Betty Robison*, *Prime Time America*, Canada's *100 Huntley Street*, *Janet Parshall's America*, *Mornings with Lorri & Larry*, FamilyNet Television and Radio, *A Time for Hope*, etc. He and his wife Katrina have three daughters and eleven grandchildren. He is also co-owner of Roan Mountain Bed and Breakfast in Roan Mountain, Tennessee (roanmountainbedandbreakfast.com).

David Potete married Pam in 1978 and has been extremely happily married all these years. He entered the ministry in 1980, and has been pastoring Northwest Community Church in Chicago since 1991. His passions are the

Gospel of Christ, cities (especially Chicago!), running, and chocolate. He earned a B.A. in business from Northeastern Illinois University in Chicago in 1981, a B.A. in Bible and Pastoral Administration from FWBBC in 1990, and an M.A. in Urban Ministry from Moody Theological Seminary in 2010.

Kevin Riggs has been married to his high-school sweetheart since 1987. The bulk of their married life has been spent in Franklin, TN, pastoring Franklin Community Church. In addition to pastoring, Kevin teaches Sociology at Nashville State Community College and Williamson Christian College. He is also an adjunct professor at Rockbridge Seminary. Kevin completed his undergraduate degree from Free Will Baptist Bible College; his Master's degree from Trevecca Nazarene University; and his Doctorate from Oxford Graduate School. His passion is to see lives transformed by the power of God's grace. Kevin has written for ONE magazine, Interlinc', the Weslyean Publishing House, David C. Cook, and Thomas Nelson Publishers. In 2007 he had his first book published by Randall House titled, *Failing Like Jesus.* Kevin loves to scuba dive and is a Divemaster with PADI (Professional Association of Diving Instructors).

Tim W. Stout, an Ohio native, is an alumnus of Free Will Baptist Bible College. In 1979, he married the former Tobianne Daniel of Kentucky and they have been blessed with three children and five grandchildren. He announced his call to preach at age 16 and was ordained in 1980 by the Cuyahoga-Lorain County Conference of Free Will Baptists in Ohio. He has served churches in West Virginia, North Carolina and Ohio. Since July of 2000, he has served as senior pastor of Heritage Free Will Baptist Church in Columbus, OH. His passion is to love God and people and stay saturated in God's Word. Tim has served Free Will Baptists on the local, state and national levels, presently serving on the Ohio State and the National Home Mission Boards.

Tommy Swindol has been in ministry since 2005 and is the Minister of Young Adults at The Donelson Fellowship in Nashville, TN. He and his wonderful wife, Jessica, have two beautiful daughters, Anna Claire and Emily. Tommy is a graduate of Free Will Baptist Bible College, Liberty University (MAR in Discipleship Ministries) and is almost done with his MDiv in Pastoral Ministry. Tommy has a passion to share God's Word and mentor the next generation. He gets the opportunity to speak all over the country and is passionate about discipleship and sharing the truths of God's Word in a relevant and challenging way.

David Trogdon was born into a Free Will Baptist pastor's home and gave his life to Christ at age six. He joined the Army when he was 17 years old and served for almost nine years. David married his sweetheart, Connie, on April 19, 1981. God blessed David and Connie with two children, Joshua and Rebekah, and four "perfect" grandchildren. David pastored Tippett's Chapel Free Will Baptist Church in Clayton, NC from 1991-2000 and has served as a Free Will Baptist Army Chaplain since 2000. David graduated from Free Will Baptist Bible College in 1991 with a B.A. in Pastoral Administration and Bible and Southeastern Southern Baptist Seminary in 1999 with an M-DIV with Biblical Languages. David's passion is to serve God and minister to soldiers and their families. David has written articles for Contact, ONE Magazine, Fusion, "The Army Chaplaincy" and "Operation Eternal Freedom" 28-day devotional Bible study.

Randy Wilson has been the senior pastor of Bethany Free Will Baptist Church in Broken Arrow, Oklahoma, since 1992. He has a B.A. degree from Hillsdale Free Will Baptist College and a M. Div. degree from Southwestern Baptist Theological Seminary. He and his wife, Donell, have been married since 1977 and have two grown children, Chris and Catie. Randy enjoys traveling, playing golf, and spending time with family and friends.

Melvin Worthington is husband to Anne and father of two grown kids, Daniel and Lydia. He was ordained in 1957 by the Ayden Free Will Baptist Church and Central Conference. He pastored in five states before becoming the Free Will Baptist executive secretary where he served for 23 years until his retirement. During his time as Free Will Baptist national leader, Melvin served in various capacities on numerous boards including American Family Association, Evangelical Press Association, Religious Conference Management Association, Randall House Board, and the Free Will Baptist Foundation Board. He wrote numerous articles and has been published in Contact, ONE Magazine, and within *The Nelson's Annual Preacher's Sourcebook* published by Thomas Nelson.

D6 Devotional Magazines
for the entire family!

   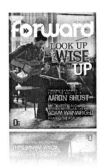 

D6 Devotional Magazines are unique because they are the only brand of devotional magazines where the entire family studies the same Bible theme at the same time.

Think about how long it would take you to track down all of the resources for each member of your family to connect with God on the same topic. Who has that kind of time? We do! It's not that we have nothing else to do, we are just passionate about D6. So look no further, we have created the resource for which you are looking, and it works!

D6 Devotional Magazines are full-color, interactive, fun, and exciting tools to connect with God and with each other.

Subscribe now!
800.877.7030
D6family.com

splink
Simple ways to Link
your family together.

it's free!

http://www.d6family.com

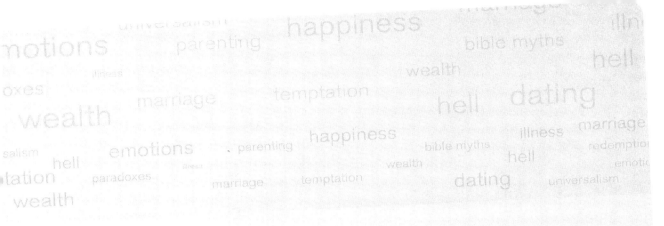  
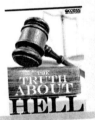    

CPSIA information can be obtained at www.ICGtesting.com
Printed in the USA
LVOW110731171012

303189LV00002B/4/P